# COURAGEOUS SURRENDER

## A PROPHETIC BLUEPRINT FOR EMPOWERED KINGDOM LIVING

## Table of Contents

# DEDICATION

To my adored King and best friend, Jesus – thank you for transforming my life and giving me the grace and hope to carry on. Your presence is more valuable to me than anything else I could ever attain in this life.

To my husband, Jeff – you are a one-of-a-kind gem. Your provision, protection, love and loyalty has surpassed anything I've know this side of heaven – It is my privilege to call you mine.

To my family and friends who have stood by me – your unwavering love, encouragement, and belief in me have carried me through some of the most difficult seasons of my life. Your support have meant more than words can express, and for that, I am forever grateful.

To my enemies who help shape me – your challenges became the fire that forged my resilience.

Thank you.

# INTRODUCTION

## THE DREAM

*"Now go and write down these words. Write them in a book. They will stand until the end of time as a witness."*
**—Isaiah 30:8 NLT**

In the early hours of October 30, 2010—4:20 a.m., to be exact—I awoke from a dream. I knew God was speaking to me about parts of my destiny. The dream had an unusual storyline with intriguing details, but it was undoubtedly prophetic.

Little did I know at the time how this dream would weave its way through my life, unfolding years later and bringing with it the manifestation and fruit of its purpose. Not fully understanding what it meant—or how my life would look as I walked through it—was a blessing in disguise. Had I realized how I would live out this prophetic dream, I might have buried my head in the sand and prayed for it to go away.

Much like Joseph, who had a dream that stirred indignation in his family, I faced incredible challenges, betrayal, pain, and delays before seeing God's plan come into focus. Yet, just as Joseph's dream unfolded according to God's timing, purpose, and plan—not only for his life but also for the benefit of his family—my God-given dream followed a similar path.

My journey, like Joseph's, unfolded in ways I could never have imagined. It was filled with twists and turns, painful experiences, and hurtful encounters. As I grew in my walk with the Lord, I came to understand that prophetic dreams and words are often meant for a time much farther down the road.

Of course, when we receive a prophetic word, our natural inclination is to believe its fulfillment is "right around the corner." We try our hardest to pull that word into the present, doing everything in our power to make it happen. Heads up: this never works! These vain attempts only delay and distract us from being fully present where God has us today.

The purpose of a prophetic word is to uncover the hidden treasure within us and to strengthen our sails when the winds blow against us, discouraging us from walking the path of our destiny. Prophetic words and dreams anchor us in our future, empowering us to endure the refining process of our journey.

God gives us the prophetic to strengthen our resolve so we press in and do not give up during preparation.

It's in this process that we become equipped to carry and steward the vision He has placed within us.

Allow me to share this God-dream with you—a prophetic picture, I believe, for every born-again believer of what the Lord desires from us: to be Kingdom-centric sons and daughters in this age of revival.

## THE DREAM

"My husband and I were at a reunion on my dad's side of the family. I had introduced him to everyone, and we were having an enjoyable time. I then saw my Aunt Jeanette, who had been battling cancer. I hugged her and started to cry. I just loved on her and continued to cry as I somehow felt the pain she was experiencing.

In the very next scene of my dream, I was at a funeral home, getting ready to be embalmed. The strange thing was, I was still alive in the dream, yet I had chosen to die. Then, I saw myself as the Funeral Director. I was both people in the dream—the one dying and the one doing the embalming and preparing the body for the funeral.

The Funeral Director said to me that it was time and approached me with a syringe. I felt extremely nervous but ready. I told the Funeral Director (Me) what a special job she had in preparing people for their family—making them look so beautiful.

Although I was ready, I felt both excited and anxious about the process of dying. I started to cry, trying to figure out how I could tell my husband one last time that I loved him. Then, I had the immediate thought to write it all down on paper for him to read.

Then, I woke up."

Have you ever had a dream so out of the box, you just knew it was from God? I've had some interesting dreams over the years, but nothing quite as unusual as this. Yet I knew, without a doubt, this was from God. It was His assignment for me: one day, I would write down what I had journeyed through so that it could help the body of Christ be better equipped to walk out their own purpose on the earth and fulfill their calling—despite the tough and sometimes daunting times they would undoubtedly face.

This book is the prophetic fulfillment of that dream and a testimony of how God weaved every detail of life's difficulties for good—not only for my growth but now for yours.

A surrendered life is not for the faint of heart, but it is for the believing heart. Friend, there will be difficult and grievous times we must walk through in this world, but my hope is that you find encouragement and boldness to be uniquely you through every struggle as you are shaped and molded into Christlikeness.

My prayer is that you will see yourself and life's challenges as seeds sown into fertile ground. As you allow those seeds to be watered by the Word of God and the counsel of the Holy Spirit, the harvest they will produce will far exceed anything you could hope for or imagine.

The byproduct of a life of surrender is this: Jesus magnified on this earth, His Kingdom impacted by your "yes," and a truly abundant life.

So, buckle your seatbelt—you are in for a ride. If you allow it, this journey, through all its ups and downs, will produce a bounty that glorifies our King and brings an abundance that not only blesses you but also leaves a generational legacy of wisdom. It will feed and nourish the lives of those in your sphere of influence.

This is a battle weapon for your arsenal, meant to help you fight the good fight of faith and storm the gates of hell, no matter the obstacles thrown your way.

Friend, you did not pick up Courageous Surrender by accident. God knows what we need and the precise timing when we are ready to lean in and learn. So, bring a teachable heart and allow the Spirit of God to breathe fresh life into your wearied soul. Let Him empower you to rise with unstoppable courage to live a set-apart life—marked by your surrender to Him.

# CHAPTER ONE

## The War Of Perseverance: Producing Growth And Maturity

*"Through Him we also have access by faith into this [remarkable state of] grace in which we [firmly and safely and securely] stand. Let us rejoice in our hope and the confident assurance of experiencing and enjoying the glory of [our great] God [the manifestation of His excellence and power]. And not only this, but with joy let us exult in our sufferings and rejoice in our hardships, knowing that hardship (distress, pressure, trouble) produces patient endurance; and endurance, proven character (spiritual maturity); and proven character, hope and confident assurance of eternal salvation."*
**—Romans 5:2-4 AMP**

Perseverance is not only a fruit—or virtue—of the Holy Spirit; it is also a mighty weapon in the spiritual war we face. Learning to wield this weapon takes practice—and plenty of it! At first, it may feel impossible to lift, let alone use effectively. You may never have had to work the spiritual "muscles" required to use this weapon, or perhaps you've had a little practice in a battle or two. Either way, you may still feel unconditioned to lift and wield this powerful weapon with skill.

The weight of perseverance will often cause fatigue, tempting you to lay it down in surrender to the enemy and his tactics, which are designed to wear you out. At times, you may even believe the lie that you cannot handle one more obstacle, disappointment, or blow to God's promises in your life. But as you train yourself, building those perseverance muscles and conditioning yourself to wield this weapon, your resilience and spiritual skill will grow. In time, the enemy will stand no chance against this dynamic, often underestimated weapon—a weapon that is key to maturing in the Spirit and establishing deep roots of faith.

This principle is true in every area of life where genuine growth is desired. If we want to build physical muscle, we must put in the work and push beyond our limits. The weights we lift when we first begin training will seem light compared to what we can handle after consistent effort. Eventually, we may plateau, requiring heavier weights, adjustments to our form, or new strategies to push past a rut.

The same is true in business. If we want to take our endeavors to the next level, we must innovate, strengthen relationships, or even invest in a mentor to help us overcome limiting beliefs. Growth—whether physical, professional, or spiritual—requires stretching, discomfort, and sometimes pain. There is no shortcut to lasting results. Muscles grow by lifting heavier weights or increasing training time. Businesses grow by stepping out of comfort zones for a stronger future. And spiritual lives grow when challenged by life's difficulties—if we do not give up.

We are made in Christ's image, and He promises to complete the good work He began in us, equipping us for our destiny. This includes the weapon of perseverance. Never underestimate the refinement that comes from perseverance, which multiplies character, hope, and confidence.

*"We have become His poetry, a re-created people that will fulfill the destiny He has given each of us, for we are joined to Jesus, the Anointed One. Even before we were born, God planned in advance our destiny and the good works we would do to fulfill it!"*
—**Ephesians 2:10 TPT**

Friend, before you were born, the Lord not only wrote your destiny but also promised to fulfill it! Your destiny is written in the Book of Life. A heavenly scroll bears your name and the fulfillment of His promises for you. This means that no matter what has come against you—no matter who has caused you pain or what the enemy of your soul has done to delay or bring sorrow—God has already written His good and perfect will for your life. His plan is unshakable, and His purpose for you is firm.

The only one who can hinder this fulfillment is you. All God requires of you is trust and your willingness to co-labor with Him. Although the process may be challenging, it is an opportunity to grow in perseverance. Each trial refines us, enabling us to mature in faith and become the spotless Bride who glorifies Jesus on this earth.

You were created for such a time as this! God placed you here, in this moment in history, with purpose. Your life, your story, and your resilience matter deeply. Even if you can't yet see the bigger picture, trust that God is working. The light at the end of the tunnel is there, and the seeds you've sown—seeds of faith, surrender, and perseverance—will yield fruit in God's perfect timing.

Allow perseverance to be forged in your heart, and you will stand as the mighty warrior God created you to be. No Goliath will stand a chance in your presence!

Perseverance is the ability to endure hardship and remain faithful to God. How do we grow in faithfulness? By growing in perseverance and steadfastness. And that growth only comes through hardship. Perseverance is forged in dark valleys and rugged terrain—not on smooth roads or mountaintop harvests. It is cultivated when seeds of surrender are planted into hard, uncertain ground, and we wait in faith for God to bring the harvest.

The process of perseverance is not for the faint of heart. It is painful and often slow. But the reward—fellowship with the Lover of your soul—is far greater than the hindrances you endure along the way. Allow perseverance to complete its work in you, refining your character, strengthening you for battle, and building in you an unmatched resilience. This resilience will confound the enemy, and you will stand as an overcomer, mighty in God's power.

Perseverance is an act of war. Don't stop. Keep pressing forward!

**DECREE WITH YOUR MOUTH:**

"I will remain steadfast. I will persevere in all things. I will wield this weapon of war, even when it hurts. I will trust God through this process of building and strengthening my character and maturity, no matter what it looks like."

# CHAPTER TWO

## Pain To Glory: The Gift That Keeps On Giving

*"The second son he named Ephraim and said, 'It is because God has made me fruitful in the land of my suffering.'"*
**—Genesis 41:52 NIV**

Pain. Ouch! The very word itself can evoke all kinds of feelings, can't it? From broken bones to broken hearts, pain runs the gamut of emotions and affects our sensitivities. Pain is something we humans naturally strive to avoid. But despite its discomfort, pain can actually produce fruit in our lives—and is something I've come to realize is a gift that keeps on giving. I am not talking about some twisted, sadistic concept of pain, but what the Scriptures tell us in the Word of God. There are many examples given that teach us that out of our pain comes life. It can produce so many things in our lives that are essential to living in the abundance of Christ. I want you to masticate this paragraph. Chew on it, digest it, and allow the nutrients of this uncommon concept to be absorbed. They will be life-giving words and refreshment to your weary soul.

Although some pain is self-inflicted because of our own disobedience and willful choices, other pain may come from the distorted hearts or hands of others. Jesus endured the feelings of pain in the garden of Gethsemane, and His pain was the result of the heart and hands of others. In this garden, He was grieved and distressed to the point of death. He even asked the Father, "If it is possible, take this cup of suffering from me." Can you feel it? Jesus foresaw what was about to take place for the redemption of mankind. He saw the transaction of His life—and all the gory details—for yours. He was the perfect, blameless sacrificial Lamb about to give up His life for you. Jesus was feeling all kinds of emotion, and I can only imagine what that may have felt like. "No, Father, I'm not ready! No, Father, I don't want to leave my mom, my family, my friends! No, Father, my life has just begun! No, Father, I don't want to experience even one minute separated from Your presence! No, Father, I don't think I can endure the pain! Father, they have rejected me, laughing at me, gossiping about me, calling me a liar and fraud. Father, I chose only to love, and now it is costing me everything!" Can you feel the distress? The sorrow? The betrayal? The intensity of living out your last moments on earth? Jesus even made three trips to pray earnestly to His Father—can you feel the pleading to not have to endure the pain of the cross?

The pain of leaving everything familiar and comfortable behind?

This necessary pain that would take our Savior through the most brutal moments of His life would ultimately lead to glory. A glory unmatched by anything else the world had seen. Glory that carried with it redemption and recompense for what was once lost. Had the devil understood there would be such purpose in the pain, he would have never influenced a single person to carry out his bidding. But the enemy is a liar and a counterfeit. He thinks he has the upper hand by inflicting pain, sorrow, and disappointment in our lives, but God! The promise you can hold onto is that if you love God, then ALL things will be turned around for your good. God is not the author of pain or evil, but if we trust Him, He will turn it on its head—and that, you can take to the bank.

Jesus tells us that in order to be a disciple, every born-again believer must take up their cross. But what does that mean exactly? It is not what some would describe as a burden you must bear, like a thorn in your side, with all the self-loathing and pity, as they say, "Oh! It's just my cross to bear." To grow in faith and discipleship, to be a learned one, to walk in the same resurrecting power and authority, we must carry a cross—and that means one thing…death—death by crucifixion. The Romans would force convicted criminals to carry their own crosses to the place of death, where they would face disgrace along the way.

*"And anyone who comes to me must be willing to share my cross and experience it as his own, or he cannot be considered to be my disciple."*
—**Luke 14:27 TPT**

To truly follow Jesus, one must be willing to carry their cross and die (self-sacrifice) to the flesh (decisions or actions made apart from faith or independent from God's working; Strongs 4561). This is the road less traveled. The road of counterculture. The road of a surrendered life so you can access (inherit) the Kingdom. Accessing the Kingdom is different from entering the Kingdom. Access is the inheritance to rulership—it is kingly authority. With all the beauty of salvation, we should not be content with just entering the Kingdom but earnestly desire to have the full inheritance of sonship and the full access that it provides. Too many in the body of Christ are content with a superficial, noncommittal relationship with Jesus. They stop short of all that Jesus died to give them and then wonder why life is so hard. They halfheartedly want to "date" Jesus while dodging the invitation to a marriage covenant. But here's the reality: dating will never provide you with the same access, privileges, and intimacy (closeness) of being married. We are called to live a yielded life, a bride surrendered to her King—a life that produces unfathomable riches and abundance; a life that trusts in the covering and protection from the God Most High so we can enjoy the fullness of our salvation.

I want to ask you: Are you carrying your cross? Have you even considered what it means? Are you on the path of surrendering your life and all its soulish repugnance that has yet to die? It will be a choice that contradicts the very systems of the world and its "do whatever makes you feel good" adage. As in my dream in the introduction of this book, I was submitted to the syringe and had chosen to die—to die to the desires of the flesh. The only way up is down. Six feet under, down. But it is a choice—a choice that results in an abundant kind of life, a God-kind of life that produces His fullness of love, power, and stability. If you want this kind of life, then the requirement is to lay your life down so that you can then be raised in greater glory. When the aspects of our flesh are dead, then our spirit can truly thrive. To be a glory carrier, death is the prerequisite.

By all definitions, pain is pain. But not all pain is equal. The greater your calling, the greater the weight of that cross will be. Meaning, you will experience unusual attacks and warfare that others will not. At times, it will feel unrelenting. As you carry that cross, it will expose a lot of areas in your life that must be yielded to God. Every step, every tear, every battle, every doubt, every fear, every unjust action against you—surrendered. Grief, sorrow, all the "why" questions—laid down. All the self-inflicted wounds from your pride and selfishness—nailed. The journey of carrying this cross is not an easy one, but a necessary one to be in intimate fellowship with the Lover of your soul. Through the process of walking with your cross, you will learn dependence on God through blood, sweat, tears, and humility. The actual journey of carrying your cross is the process of submitting and trusting God with the things that are revealed to you in your suffering. It is the path of no reputation.

On the cross, what happened to Jesus? He died, but through His death, He was raised and now lives! He was resurrected and sits at the right hand of the Father. His pain was turned into greater glory! We often pray to know Jesus better and earnestly desire to walk in the power and authority He gave us and to see signs, miracles, and wonders in our lives and ministry. But we rarely, if ever, consider the cost. We admire the men and women of God who are being used mightily, especially in the public arena—but we seldom consider what that anointing cost them to carry. You have no idea! The oil (anointing) is extremely expensive—it will cost you everything! But the cost comes with a promise: as we are one with Jesus in His death, so will we be in His resurrection. And in the death, we will experience the overflowing power of Him working in us. There is no shortcut. The cross you carry will produce suffering. However, the outcome is the reward of oneness with God, becoming one perfect man with the full dimensions of spiritual maturity.

*"And I continually long to know the wonders of Jesus more fully and to experience the overflowing power of His resurrection working in me. I will be one with Him in His sufferings and I will be one with Him in His death. Only then will I be able to experience complete oneness with Him in His resurrection from the realm of death."*
**—Philippians 3:10 TPT**

This chapter is to help you see more clearly that your pain is only a catalyst to the glory you will walk in. We are promised to go from glory to glory, which is God's infinite worth. Every challenging thing will be upgraded to glory if you faint not. That is how our pain is turned into a gift. And because pain is inevitable in this life, it is a gift that can keep on giving, producing fruit that honors God and benefits us and those in our realm of influence.

*"And that's not all. We also celebrate in seasons of suffering because we know that when we suffer, we develop endurance, which shapes our characters. When our characters are refined, we learn what it means to hope and anticipate God's goodness. And hope will never fail to satisfy our deepest need because the Holy Spirit that was given to us has flooded our hearts with God's love."*
**—Romans 5:3 The Voice**

As real as our pain is, it is shrouded in disguise. Pain hurts! It starts off looking only as this horrible, useless emotion with no benefit. It will cause us to believe that what we have endured was an absolute waste of our existence. We rarely have the foresight to see the healing that can come from our pain, but healing is the end result when something is restored. And Jesus is a Restorer! Consider the pain of a broken bone. It's excruciating and takes weeks, if not months, to heal. But it does eventually mend, doesn't it? As we submit these experiences to God and His Kingship to flip the unflippable, we become image bearers of Christ on this earth. Where our sufferings are turned into unspeakable glory—His glory refines us in our pain and unveils in us unlimited riches, favor, and supernatural strength in our innermost being with His might and power.

*"I have refined you, but not as silver is refined.*
*Rather, I have refined you in the furnace of suffering.*
*I will rescue you for my sake—yes, for my own sake!*
*I will not let my reputation be tarnished, and I will*
*not share my glory with idols!"*
**—Isaiah 48:10 TPT**

Dear reader, there is reward beyond your pain. You must believe this. God is faithful. His love endures forever. And although He never authorizes evil, He will pull out the treasures in us despite the enemy's schemes to harm us and destroy our hope. If we allow the finished work of the cross to have its way in our lives, completing the work in us, everything we are allowed to experience, He will resurrect and breathe life on once again. But a seed not sown can never produce, not a single plant or a mighty oak tree. Sowing our pain can be something we resist because, frankly, we want to control the outcome, feeling justified in our response. We inadvertently fall into the trap of believing the lie that our "feelings," or self-preservation, are somehow warranted as we convince ourselves that we can control the narrative of our lives or those around us. We hold onto the delusion that we have the power to magically prevent our suffering.

First off, control is always rooted in fear, and choosing it will only delay the inevitable of producing the greater glory in our lives. What I have learned through many years of challenges is that our feelings have nothing to do with trusting God; they have nothing to do with forgiveness. Harboring bitterness only keeps us in bondage. A hardened, unforgiving heart not only prevents you from hearing God and walking out your destiny, but it will give the enemy legal access to your life. It truly causes spiritual turmoil that will hinder your growth and even impact the lives of your household. Instead, allow the transforming work of God in your heart by His supernatural grace to take the graveyard of your pain and resurrect it with purpose and glory. It will surpass anything you had ever hoped for or could imagine. That is our God.

# CHAPTER THREE

## The Im*POSSIBLE*: Trusting God

*"Trust in the Lord with all your heart and lean not on your own understanding; in all your ways submit to him, and he will make your paths straight."*
**—Proverbs 3:5-6 NIV**

Trusting the Almighty seems like an easy thing to do, doesn't it? I mean, after all, He is God! The uncreated Creator. The One who spoke the Universe into existence. King Solomon, who wrote the wise counsel in Proverbs, clearly instructs us to not only trust, but to trust the Lord with everything we've got. As Christians, we read and decree this verse all the time; some of us may even have the scripture displayed on the walls of our homes as a reminder. And I believe at a fundamental level, Christians do understand the importance of trusting God. I mean, why wouldn't we trust the One we gave our lives to—the One we know holds all authority in the palm of His hands?! Sure, we say, "I can trust You, God, with all my heart."

Then, something earth-shattering and life-altering happens. God shakes our lives up a bit, and we experience things that destroy our storyline. Our God, Yahweh, allows us to be sifted, as Job was, and we suddenly experience loss. The things we held onto so dearly seemingly peel out of our hands. We begin to convince ourselves—or maybe someone close to us has our ear—and tells us how God would never do that! God would never allow that to happen to me! We battle with a lie that somehow God would spare us from discomfort. Because, hey! This life is about me and my goals, my dreams, my ambitions, my pleasure. My life is supposed to be pain-free and easy sailing. Or we go in the other direction and fall into self-righteous drive, telling ourselves how good we've been and how much we've done for the Kingdom. You know what I'm talking about, don't you? Lord, but I've sacrificed for You! Look at all I've done for You, as we list off XYZ. Spouting off how this shakeup is not supposed to be a part of our story and how unfair this is! And yet when you read the Bible, you see how that is not true. The life we are called to live is a life laid down; a life that carries its own cross; a life that is no longer ours but given to the One who paid a costly price for it. We need to understand the reality that living a surrendered life will mean experiencing hard things. Why? Because when our hope is in Christ, hard things build character and perseverance. Hard things refine us in the fiery furnace as they burn off the dross to reveal the purity of gold in us, which ultimately allows us to reflect the image of Jesus to a dying and hurting world around us.

It's much easier to sing hallelujah when we are skipping through life and whistling Dixie. "Praise the Lord" this and "praise the Lord" that. But what happens deep in your soul when life is turned upside down? When you are crushed by the weight of pain? Your whistle fizzles. Your hope crashes. Your mind spins out of control. You find yourself bombarded with fear and creating scenarios of the worst possible outcome. You grab the lie, like Adam and Eve did, that your heavenly Father is not who He said He is. Questioning His Word, His promises, His best for your life. We allow the shifty serpent to whisper in our ears that God is not for us, because hey, if He were, He surely would save you from these hard and painful things. All lies! As sons and daughters of the Most High, you have got to determine for yourself, at the core of who you are, that Christ is for you. You have to decide what you believe: God is either trustworthy, or He's a liar. There is no middle ground. It is one or the other, and despite how much you try to candy-coat it, your core belief will get exposed in the turbulent cycles of life. And when it does, it's an opportunity to repent and grow in greater trust in the Lord.

The truth is that God's promise is that ALL THINGS work for your benefit and His glory for those who BELIEVE. It does not matter if you understand His ways. It does not matter if His methods make you uneasy. His plan and purpose for our lives are not dependent on our ability to figure out what He's doing. Quite frankly, understanding can be overrated. I knew a man years ago in ministry who was full of logic. He was all about thinking more. And although we are living in a time where not enough people use their critical thinking skills, his "thinkology" (is that a word? lol) was, frankly, exhausting. I don't doubt this man loved Jesus but in my experience, there was no balance of heart, which left you feeling void of spirit. It was to the point of overthinking everything you said, to the degree of being completely unreliant on the Holy Spirit and consumed with your own ideologies of how something should be done or said.

God's ways are higher than ours, and we will never fully understand how He chooses to work things out. So, take a breath. It is okay not to know. All you need to do is trust Him and His process to complete the work He's begun in you. I understand how trusting God through the trials and struggles in life may seem impossible, especially when we walk through the valley of death—or through deserts of dryness when God seems silent. But He is fully and completely trustworthy. His plans for you are perfect. His desire for you is to bear much fruit and grow in maturity in the things of the Spirit so you can reflect His image. He knows what He is doing. Do you know that your trust in the Lord (no matter what things look or feel like) is not only credited to you as righteousness, but it pleases Him?

*"And Abram believed the Lord, and the Lord declared him righteous because of his faith."*
**—Genesis 15:6 NLT**

*"And it is impossible to please God without faith. Anyone who wants to come to Him must believe that God exists and that He rewards those who sincerely seek Him."*
**—Hebrews 11:6 NLT**

Hebrews 11:6 has always carried so much power for me. Truly, I can remember soaking in this verse from my earliest years as a 24-year-old new believer and follower of Christ. I would think, "Wow! God, just having faith in You pleases You? That's it? I can do that! I can believe You!" My heart, from the time I said yes to Jesus, was always to please Him. I would say, "You know what, Lord, I might get things wrong, I might screw things up, I will undoubtedly fail You, but...I can surely have faith that pleases You." And there are many people in my life who can attest that I certainly have been a woman of faith—stubborn faith, to be more exact. Faith that digs her heels in and has withstood the strongest of storms. Little did I know just how much that desire—that faith I wanted to walk in to trust Jesus, to please my God—would be tested, over and over and over again. It was like God would say to Satan, "Go ahead, sift her and see what she's made of!"

Now, with that said, that does not mean I've managed to always walk out my faith without the tension of experiencing doubt. As we grow in the Lord and as we are advancing in our calling and purpose, the intensity of opposition that may be allowed to really put our faith to the test will happen. Sorry, I wish I could say it's all rainbows and butterflies, but new levels of advancement—and simply being mature—requires new levels of training, which usually means deeper surrender and healing. I've been hit pretty hard by circumstances that could easily throw even the most resilient into despair. Maybe you can relate, and you feel like raising the white flag. Those times of growth for me have sometimes been a real doozy, if you know what I mean. Like crawling into a hole and disappearing kind of doozy—"Give me a cave, O God, and let the ravens feed me." Like the life just got sucked out of me and hit me with a whirlwind of sadness, doozy. During these times of intensity, I have had to humble myself and expose my vulnerability, asking for prayer—for my family to literally lay hands on me because I had nothing left in me to fight as the sadness overtook me. The process of some of these life experiences was grueling and took time to overcome. I had to choose to press through as I was challenged with what I had always believed to be true. Did I believe what I always professed to believe? Is Jesus the same yesterday, today, and forever? Does God really know what He's doing? Was this God's punishment? Did I do something to deserve this kind of pain? Was I a horrible mother, daughter, sister, friend? All these questions circled my heart and my mind as I attempted to cast down every vain imagination and bring into captivity every thought. At times, I was in such despair that I couldn't even be around people because my sadness was just too great. But in my surrender, something finally shifted. In my surrender—in case you missed it—this is a key for you to hold onto.

As I pressed in, praying in the Spirit, because I had no logical words to convey the pain or how to even begin to process what I was experiencing, the Holy Spirit began counseling me, comforting me. He reminded me of the Truth. The grace of God began to lift me up, and I was once again able to put my battle fatigues back on and do what I knew to do. I went to war over my destiny and that of loved ones. I began decreeing all that is good and true over myself and those that caused so much pain to my heart. I began once again believing that God is trustworthy. When I began seeing with the eyes of Jesus and His perspective, instead of the confusion, lies, and the snare of offense that comes from the enemy, I knew the faith I had always carried was increased a few notches. As the fog cleared and I was able to regain my footing, I began understanding the purpose of this testing in my life was about me more than about the ones who caused me the pain. It was part of my story and what God would use to grow my character and reflection of Jesus and to be trusted with what He would place in my hands. The enemy thought he could destroy me, and honestly, at times, it felt he was going to succeed. The distraction from deep sorrow and pain will cause you to lose focus of what is true. But God had greater plans for my destiny! He already placed in me everything I needed to overcome; I just had to remember how to access it. I understand now that all of this was a test of trust. Was I going to believe the truth that my God is trustworthy even through the most difficult, painful times of my life? If I could not stand in the faith that I professed—the faith that pleases God—then how could I trust Him for the greater works, the impossible things yet to come?

I have learned through this journey that trusting God is always the best choice! Any other option is simply foolish! It only causes more stress and delays our purpose on this earth. If you think about it, it makes zero sense to question our God. God is for you! God's plan for your life will be fulfilled, and no person or demon can stop it! The only one that has the power to dismantle and delay your purpose is you. What seems impossible is just a façade. Don't fall for it. The next time you experience doubt through some crazy attempt of the enemy to waylay your destiny, do yourself a huge favor and quickly kick it to the curb. Do not allow that shifty serpent to enter your thoughts—don't entertain what is not from God. God is not a man that He would lie! Period. Satan is the father of lies. Who will you believe when the going gets tough? Your peace and your process depend on this choice.

Instead of spiraling out of control and sitting in the pit of hopelessness, begin declaring who God says He is. Decree His Lordship over your life. Decree that the beginning of wisdom is the fear of the Lord and in God, you will trust and not be afraid. Decree that you are like an olive tree flourishing in the house of God. Decree that you will trust in Him at all times because He is your refuge and there is no one like Him. Decree, "You, O God, will answer my prayers because I place my trust in You." Declare that God will plead your case among the unfaithful and rescue you from the deceitful. Decree that He will vindicate you and declare your innocence. Declare that it is He who will shut the mouths of lions and bring about your justice. Decree the prodigal is coming home. Decree healing, restoration, and recompense of all that was stolen. Decree unity and wholeness over your family. This is what is pleasing and acceptable to the Lord—trusting Him and being obedient to His Word.

Will you do this? Will you make a commitment to stand on the living Word of God? Will you take the challenge of declaration over you and your household, not just when it's convenient but when it's hard? Will you rattle the gates of hell with your decision to stand and trust your God in the face of opposition and doubt? Use your voice as a trumpet and blow that horn!

# CHAPTER FOUR

## Victory Of Identity: Laying A Foundation

*"Let me illustrate: As long as an heir is a minor, he's not really much different than a servant, although he's the master over all of them. For until the time appointed by the father, the child is under the domestic supervision of the guardians of the estate. So it is with us. When we were juveniles, we were enslaved under the hostile spirits of the world. But when the time of fulfillment had come, God sent his Son, born of a woman, born under the law. Yet all of this was so that he would redeem and set free those held hostage to the law, so that we would receive our freedom and a full legal adoption as his children. And so that we would know that we are his true children, God released the Spirit of Sonship into our hearts— moving us to cry out intimately, 'My Father! My true Father!' Now we're no longer living like slaves under the law, but we enjoy being God's very own sons and daughters! And because we're his, we can access everything our Father has—for we are heirs because of what God has done!"*
**—Galatians 4:1-7 TPT**

### ID Please!

Do you know who you are? I mean, really know who you are? Not just your name or title, but as a Believer who confesses Jesus as Lord, do you know who He says you are? You are a child of the Most High, adopted into the family of God (**Ephesians 1:5**); a citizen of heaven (**Ephesians 2:19**); seated in heavenly places (**Ephesians 2:6**); co-crucified and co-heirs with Christ, with full kingdom inheritance (**Galatians 2:20, Romans 8:17, Matthew 25:34**). This is the identity I am talking about! If you do not know THIS identity, you will undoubtedly act, in one way or another, like a spiritual orphan. And the Church today is full of spiritual orphans who do not have any idea who God says they are. Instead, they are confused, stumbling all over the place, full of fleshly responses to doing life, and battling daily offense and bitterness, which hinders their growth.

I am going to say a hard truth right here: You will never move in the abundance God has for you if you remain an orphan. It is crucial to understand your identity and inheritance so you can walk in the fullness of being a co-heir with Jesus. I want to equip you with understanding so you can embrace your new identity—and prosper in all ways.

The Webster Dictionary describes an orphan as: a child deprived of one or both parents, one deprived of protection or advantage. Wow! Deprivation of care, protection, and advantage. If you are not someone who has experienced neglect or absentee parents, you probably know someone who has. The good news is, we have a God—a heavenly Father—that the Bible refers to in *Daniel 5* as Abba Father—a colloquial term of familiarity that a young child would use, similar to papa or daddy—who provides all the care, protection, guidance, discipline, and favor in your life. His love is unmatched by any earthly love—even from the best parents in the world. There is no lack of any good thing for those in Christ.

You may even profess to know God as "Father," but experience an internal contradiction to that. Deep down, you may struggle to really understand just how much God loves you and who He says you are as a child of His. People who have not had healthy relationships with their own Dad tend to struggle the most with this contradiction. The world systems want to convince you otherwise, as they push an agenda for you to believe your identity is in your race, the color of your skin, your politics, or your gender. All a BIG FAT LIE! Your identity is not in anything apart from Him—He is the vine, you are the branch. He is your very source of life and your whole identity!

Do you struggle to let go and release feelings of abandonment, depression, fear, rejection, trauma, or unworthiness? If so, these emotions will keep you from receiving the Truth of who He is and how He feels about you because "feelings" do not alter the Truth. When a Believer struggles with their true God-given identity, the result is an orphan spirit. This spirit can drive a person to be manipulative and problematic, suffer from addictions, failed relationships, fear of getting close to others, or even incessantly put other people down so they feel better about themselves. The greatest consequence of walking in an orphan spirit is the raging battle to believe God's promises are for you.

Here are some characteristics of an orphan spirit:

- Always looking for the bigger, better, shinier thing
- Feelings-based faith (If it feels good, then I will believe or follow through)
- The constant need for recognition
- Easily offended
- Feelings of abandonment
- Opposes authority
- Unteachable (always knows everything)
- Survivalist mentality (always looking out for oneself)
- Poverty mindset (lack of generosity, belief that you will always be broke or not worthy of success, or anything good; fear of not having enough or hoarding money and material things)
- Rejects others before they can reject you

- Church hopping (always looking to have your ears tickled)
- Never comfortable in the presence of anointed spiritual fathers/mothers

The orphan spirit always has a love deficit that will bring about triggers by those closest to them—family, friends, or workplace colleagues. These triggers bring about distorted views of people. When you feel disregarded by parents, disrespected by spouses, dishonored by children, or dismissed by co-workers, it can be easy to begin questioning your worth or abilities. When you feel and respond out of these distorted views of others, it can also be a predominant trigger that leads to offense. This is why being grounded in the Word of God and knowing what He says about you is so important to your spiritual identity and growth. It's a bedrock to your foundation so you can mature in the Spirit and make wise choices that honor God.

When you do not know you are loved or valued, you will find it difficult to receive love or give it away without an ulterior motive. An orphan often forms a hard heart, causing resistance to Truth and love. There may even be battles with insecurity, which leads to low self-esteem, causing you to be argumentative and feel the need to be right about everything. But God loves us, not because we are good, but because His love makes us good. His way is a better way—the only fulfilling way of life and purpose.

You are the only person responsible for you and your feelings. Too many buy into the lie that others can make us feel a certain way, but feelings can be very deceptive, and a feeling of being inferior cannot happen without your permission. But if you do not know and rest in who God says you are, then the minute someone does not agree with you or says something unkind, you will become highly reactionary, even spiraling out of control. In those moments, you step out of Truth and into a lie. You are the one who needs to take ownership of what you are feeling and how you react to the hard things in your life. You do have a choice!

In the season of hard things, how we choose to respond reveals what is hidden in the recesses of our own hearts. You can believe the lies, or you can believe the truth that you have worth and love because God says so! He loves you with an everlasting love. The kind of love that was worth the life of His own Son. Knowing the power and promise of God's word will help you to be more Christlike—reflecting the image of Him who created you. This promise, along with friendship with the Holy Spirit, will help you grow and mature in your everyday life.

Having His word embedded in our heart is not optional. If we want fellowship with our heavenly Father and grow in intimacy in our relationship with Jesus, then we need to be diligent in our pursuit of knowing Him. His Word is living and active, so allow it to feed your spirit and renew your mind. God loves you right where you are at and is as close as the breath you breathe—He is the *ruach* (Hebrew word for breath, wind, spirit—**Genesis 1:2**). But He also loves you enough that He will not allow you to stay where you are; His ways are always forward-moving and are forever transforming us into His image. That is why the Bible says He takes us from glory to glory. We are a true work in progress! But for Him to complete this work, we must choose to submit to His leadership in our life.

And frankly, it is not always comfortable to let go and let Him be God. We somehow hold onto the golden calf called self and embrace the delusion of believing we can make it without Him. If you are not healing emotionally and mentally, you are not growing spiritually. There is a time to be a child and then a time to grow up. If you have been walking with Jesus for years and are still crawling around and talking like a two-year-old, offended by everything, then there is a problem with your willingness to yield to God.

I encourage you to spend some time in repentance and asking the Lord why you are afraid to surrender—it may be your fear of vulnerability, or it may be a spirit of pride that needs to be broken. Whatever the reason, renounce it and decree, *Not my will, but Your will, Lord.*

It's also important to remember that love is correction as much as it is affirmation. It requires yielding to His Spirit in your journey, obeying Him, trusting Him, and having a teachable spirit. Even when it's uncomfortable or things look quite different from what you hoped for, you still yield to His leadership in your life. Yes, even when outcomes are met with disappointment, He is always a good, good Father. That truth never changes.

As you embrace your sonship—your true identity—walking in a place of trust with your heavenly Father becomes a breeze. Loving yourself for who He created you to be becomes easier. Not being offended by others becomes less challenging. Loving others, especially the unlovable, requires less effort. But it all begins with learning who He says you are, and for that to happen, you must meditate upon His Word, getting it deep inside of you, so that you can recall and remind yourself of the Truth that not only sets you free—but will keep you free.

This is where the victory of your identity is established and the key to your destiny. Until Peter saw himself as a rock, he was not able to rise above his limiting beliefs to fulfill his mandate on the earth.

**Prayer:**

Father, I am sorry for the times in my life that I do not recognize and embrace the truth of my relationship to You—that I am Your deeply loved, fully forgiven, totally accepted child and heir to Your Kingdom with full access to everything that is Yours. I repent for responding like a juvenile that succumbs to the spirits of this world and becomes reactionary to my unyielded flesh. Give me the grace to grow in the area of sonship and to truly receive the revelation of what it means to be Yours.

CHAPTER FIVE

## Getting Out Of Neutral: Mindsets Matter

*"Stop imitating the ideals and opinions of the culture
around you, but be inwardly transformed by the Holy
Spirit through a total reformation of how you think.
This will empower you to discern God's will as you
live a beautiful life, satisfying and perfect in His
eyes."*
**—Romans 12:2 TPT**

Getting out of neutral and into gear starts with
addressing the battle between our ears—that being the
mind! Our mind is a powerful gift from God and can
be full of what is good and true, or consumed with
what is bad and lies. Our actions and thoughts will
always line up with what we believe. If you do not
know what God says in the Holy Scriptures or who He
says you are, you will always question Him when the
enemy comes whispering in your ear, and nobody is
exempt. It is every Believer's responsibility to renew
their minds so they can then be transformed by the
power and virtue of the Holy Spirit. Mind renewal is
not an option if you want to grow in strength and
character and be equipped as a powerful vessel of God.
The first step in being in alignment with God's will for
your life is to first know His Word. The Bible is the

essential tool that provides us wisdom and knowledge to mature as true sons and daughters of God. It is the only way to clean up our stinkin' thinkin'! To say it has not been one of the toughest things to learn how to overcome is an understatement. But through all my life's challenges and growth opportunities, the Spirit of the Lord has been such an amazing teacher. Truly, He has taught me the meaning of being an overcomer through the renewing of my mind.

An "overcomer" holds fast to their faith in Christ and does not turn away in times of difficulty but learns to have complete dependence upon God for strength, courage, and direction. Believers have the power, through the Holy Spirit, to overcome any attacks of the enemy (**Romans 8:35-39**). The Apostle Paul tells us to demolish every deceptive thought. Some translations say "imaginations." What you think and entertain in your thought life has great power over whether you are an overcomer or an undergoer. Trust me, an overcomer is a much better position to be in. I love how The Passion Translation words it below:

*"We can demolish every deceptive fantasy that opposes God and break through every arrogant attitude that is raised up in defiance of the true knowledge of God. We capture, like prisoners of war, every thought and insist that it bow in obedience to*

*the Anointed One. Since we are armed with such dynamic weaponry, we stand ready to punish any trace of rebellion as soon as you choose complete obedience."*
**—2 Corinthians 10:5 TPT**

Many years ago, we were facing a court battle with people who had defrauded us in a business purchase. This was a very costly battle that took years to get through. It hindered our entire lives emotionally and financially and put tremendous stress on our marriage. If that were not enough, we went through several law firms before landing the two lawyers that would see us through to the end. What a process! Through this battle of what felt like excruciating testing, I was bombarded by all kinds of thoughts and fears. How would we pay the next grocery bill, let alone replenish our lawyer's retainer? Would these people who deceived us be able to take our home? Thoughts of every worst-case scenario raced through my mind. I had to get it together and put my faith where my mouth was. Literally! If my mind was going to deliver the negative, I would have to deliver the positive with my words.

Despite how scary this battle we were facing was, I submitted this entire ordeal to God and knew He had a plan—however, my husband was not so understanding of the peace I was choosing to walk in. He thought I was "nuts!" and told me so on more than one occasion. He simply could not make sense of this peace I had. I should add here that although my husband was a Believer, he did not have the level of faith I had. He, too, was walking out his journey with God. But through every doubt and every obstacle that would try dictating the opposite of what I believed, I had to make a choice and resist those mind hurdles—some that were unrelenting. There is no good thing in putting our focus on unhealthy and unproductive thoughts, and lies are counterproductive to God's truth. So, do yourself a favor and just STOP it!

One of our lawyers was this feisty Jewish woman named Marlene. She was a tough straight-shooter and did not mince words, but I loved her frankness. I recall riding in the elevator with her one morning, and she said to me, "I'm not so sure the outcome you guys want is going to be in your favor—you need to be more realistic in your expectations." I replied, "Jesus will be with us in court, and He's promised us victory, and we will win this case!" Marlene's reply to me was, "Well, I haven't seen Jesus show up in court yet, so I'm not so sure about that!" Marlene followed her reply with a half-hearted laugh. At the end of this court battle, you guessed it, we won! I may never know if that outcome had any impact on Marlene or her faith, but Jesus received the glory that day.

Although I have many stories in my journey with God, this was just one that caused my faith to soar. The process taught me how to wage war against the constant bombardment of lies that came against us and how to leap over those mental hurdles. Our faith is not made resilient in the easy times—it is made in the trials and struggles of life. I had to learn and put into practice, often daily, to resist the devil. In so doing, he had to flee! That is God's promise. Understand that we do not fight against flesh and blood, so my husband was not the problem, nor were any family or friends that were doubters. But I did have to learn how to resist their attacks or the rolling of the eyes over my faith and declarations of victory. In the process, I also began learning how to resist offense.

You are in training to run the race. If you are experiencing mind hurdles of your own that cause you to be stuck and going nowhere, hold onto God's promises. Learn to jump over every hurdle with declarations of victory and stand on what you know to be true NO MATTER WHAT the process looks like. We can trust Him even when things do not make sense or look the way we hoped they would. Our God is a loving Father, and He knows what He's doing.

*"So if you're serious about living this new resurrection life with Christ, act like it. Pursue the things over which Christ presides. Don't shuffle along, eyes to the ground, absorbed with the things right in front of you. Look up, and be alert to what is going on around Christ—that's where the action is. See things from His perspective."*
—**Colossians 3:1-2 MSG**

I found this definition of hurdle quite fitting: A race in which a series of such barriers must be jumped without the competitors' breaking their stride. (The American Heritage Dictionary)

Do not break your stride! Stay in the race and leap over every one of those barriers by declaring God's promises. And if you stumble in the race, then pick yourself up and get back in the game. It is the truth that sets you free from every hurdle in life. It is part of your equipping, and although your purpose will generate resistance, settle it now in your mind and know that you got this!

# CHAPTER SIX

## Threshing Floor: Refinement In The Crushing

*"But they do not know the Lord's thoughts or understand His plan. These nations don't know that He is gathering them together to be beaten and trampled like sheaves of grain on a threshing floor."*
—**Micah 4:12 NLT**

We do not typically hear the words "threshing floor" in our modern vocabulary today, nor is one used anymore as an agricultural tool. However, you'll find these words in the book of Genesis, describing a process of harvesting wheat. So, what is a threshing floor, exactly?

A threshing floor is a place where people or animals were used to separate grain from the chaff — in other words, to separate the outer parts of the grain, the covering, and the debris of the seed that were useless. It was a process of sifting the grain from the chaff by beating or driving it out. After the grain was beaten and the hull loosened, the farmer would toss the grains into the air, allowing the wind to assist in blowing away the chaff. Quite a picture, and certainly helpful in understanding the meaning behind it when used as a parable in the lives of God's people. Now, with that foundation laid, allow me to help bring understanding to its deeper spiritual significance.

A follower of Jesus is someone who is genuinely walking with Him in fellowship and obeying Him. Jesus said in the Book of John, "If you love Me, you will obey Me." As we walk in this intimate place of union with God, He begins to refine us, as I've mentioned in previous chapters, for the purpose of reflecting Christ in us. This process will take you to the threshing floor, my friend — a place of sifting the righteous from the wicked things in your life. It is a place of separation, purification, and divine encounters. A place where trials and testing are allowed in your life to strip away that which is profane or useless, leaving only what is true and lasting. It is a time to embrace moments of pain and trust God to use them for our refinement and growth — turning our trials into altars of worship and transformation.

What are your unresolved heart issues? Do you find yourself with a hardened heart, unable to forgive others? What about holding onto offense, anger, or bitterness? Do you resist difficulty in your life head-on, or do you run in the other direction? What about resisting putting God first in your life? These are things that are useless debris or chaff in your heart —

the hardened shell that covers the treasure inside, waiting to be unwrapped.

You may have a valid reason for feeling the way you do, but as a son or daughter of God, you do not have the right to hold onto any of it. None of these things align with the heart of God; they only keep you locked in a prison of your own mind that prevents you from walking out and fulfilling your destiny. Issues of the heart will prevent you from growing spiritually and make it increasingly difficult to discern the voice of God. In His magnificence and righteousness, God knows this and desires to help you reposture your heart, so you can reflect the goodness of Him that now resides in you. To be about His Kingdom and His righteousness, so that all other things will be added to you. To do so requires this threshing floor process, where there is refinement in the crushing.

*"I'm baptizing you here in the river, turning your old life in for a kingdom life. The real action comes next: The main character in this drama — compared to Him, I'm a mere stagehand — will ignite the kingdom life within you, a fire within you, the Holy Spirit within you, changing you from the inside out. He's going to clean house — make a clean sweep of your lives. He'll place everything true in its proper place before God; everything false He'll put out with the*

*trash to be burned."*
**—Matthew 3:12 MSG**

God's workmanship in your life has meaning and great purpose. For us to live the kingdom life, we must allow ourselves, in submission to God's will, to be placed on His potter's wheel and transformed. This is the place where the hard and rough edges are smoothed, our character honed, and our pain, hardship, and grief can be transformed into greater grace and empowerment. When we are in control, we are always limited. But when we relinquish the false safety of control to His Lordship, we have unlimited access to the wonderful works that only He can do through the power of the Holy Spirit in us. Allow the exposure of those bitter places in you to be taken out in the trash and burned up. He's the only one who can do the most amazing transformative work in us — let Him clean house!

When you understand the purpose of crushing, you will more quickly yield to His plan and allow the hard but necessary work to begin. When you received Jesus as Lord of your life, you were instantly justified by the blood of Jesus. But your soul, on the other hand, must be regenerated. This is the work of sanctification. It is an ongoing process, from death to life, bitter to sweet, ashes to beauty — a healing and maturing of our soul. Manifesting the fruit of the Holy Spirit in our lives should be our heart's earnest desire and is essential during times of great testing. The fruit of love, joy, peace, patience, kindness, goodness, faithfulness, gentleness, and self-control must grow deeply within, forming a strong root system that will take us to new levels of maturity. Surrendering to this will leave a sweet fragrance unto the Lord, an aroma that will attract those in your circle of influence.

This is the place of separation, where being made set apart brings purity and holiness to your life. It's the place that allows you to choose what you will do when you are thrown on the threshing floor and about to be trampled underfoot, so only that which is good is left, as He allows the wind of the Holy Spirit to blow away all that is of no benefit. Then He gathers the outcasts and the afflicted and makes them into a remnant, a great nation redeemed from the hand of their enemies.

Your threshing floor is only to remove the bad and unclean things from your heart and mind. It is the place to trust that our Father God knows what He is doing. And although it will hurt for a season, the season will end. It is a place of submission to our God to make us a bride ready for her Groom, King Jesus. The first and greatest commandment is found in the book of Matthew: to love the Lord your God with all your heart, soul, and mind. The only way we can walk in this kind of love is to first be sifted on the threshing floor of separation and refined by the Refiner's fire.

As you begin to grow and mature with the understanding of God's purposes and plans for your life, embracing the truth that He has plans to prosper you and not harm you — to give you a hope and a future — you will more fully embrace the process of being sifted. You may still be white-knuckling through the process, but you will lean in, trusting His goodness, knowing He is faithful. You will more quickly look at people and events in your life through the eyes of Jesus, and instead of pointing fingers and walking in dark attitudes, you will ask, "What is going on in my heart, and what do You want to teach me, Lord, in this season of my life?" That is where real growth blooms and manifests in our lives.

On this threshing floor, you will learn to be a person of prayer — one who prays and decrees the solution, not the problem. A person who does not live by their feelings but lives in the realm of the Spirit, according to His Word, where Jesus' love will pierce your heart.

*"Those whom I [dearly and tenderly] love, I tell their faults and convict and convince and reprove and chasten [I discipline and instruct them]. So be enthusiastic and in earnest and burning with zeal and*

*repent [change your mind and attitude]."*
**—Revelation 3:19 AMP**

God's love does not look like goosebumps, but like our wrongs being exposed. His love, through this threshing floor experience, will identify the reasons why you have fear instead of faith, why you blame everyone and everything around you instead of taking ownership of your own unhealed soul. God shows His love to us by purifying us, as His Word divides soul from spirit and judges our thoughts and attitudes of the heart. Through this deep work of the heart, the outcome is we get to experience Him in ways we never thought possible, and our prayers become less and less hindered. You will learn to rise above external problems as you become more acquainted with the Lord's promises and processes of maturing us for the return of our King. As you grow in your relationship with Jesus, trusting Him wholeheartedly, your spirit becomes more sanctified and set apart, allowing you to resist more quickly anything that comes at you because you are now firmly grounded in your identity and rulership as a son or daughter. This is a powerful truth that will not only alter your journey but allow you the God-confidence to be the overcomer you were created to be — a subduer of every demonic obstacle put in your path. Declare with your mouth right now: "I AM A SUBDUER OF OBSTACLES!" Hallelujah!

# CHAPTER SEVEN

## Deep Dive: Inner Healing

*"...and the truth will set you free."*
— **John 8:32 ESV**

Have you ever considered the importance of your inner healing? The crucial role it plays in your spiritual growth and maturity? Many do not realize the significance of their soul health (mind, will, emotions). Instead, they focus on what everyone else needs, what's wrong with them, and what they need to change. Let's face it, it's just easier to point fingers than to believe there could be anything wrong with us, right? Pride is a great deceiver! And yes, pride is what keeps us from looking inward. We must be willing to push through the façade and allow Jesus to mend our hearts so we can then become healing agents to those around us, reflecting Christ in us. Without doing this deep dive of personal transformation, we will never be the whole person Jesus died for us to be.

One cannot effectively minister from a heart of purity when they are walking blindly in their pain. They will inevitably respond out of a wrong spirit, which, in turn, brings more pain, dysfunction, and confusion to the lives of those around them—especially their family. We see this all the time as parents parent from their junk rather than their treasure. Instead of leaving a legacy of life, they leave a trail of broken hearts, confused minds, and toxic belief systems that transcend their lineage—broken pieces and bondage that leave a trail of dysfunction, curses, and pain. Not the legacy anyone wants to leave for their children and grandchildren. The choice is ours! We can choose to draw the line in the sand and say, "It stops here"—surrendering our very lives at the altar and saying yes to Jesus and our own healing and deliverance.

I hope to help you understand several things in your own inner healing journey. To do that, I will begin by explaining what false perceptions are, because they lay the groundwork for why we often move into offense in our relationships. It is also the underlying reason we can stay stuck in our unhealed emotions and beliefs about ourselves and others.

Before I continue, let me be clear: not all perceptions are false. There are experiences people have endured that are not their fault and may not carry any false interpretations of what happened to them. However, even from a truthful situation, skewed beliefs and feelings about oneself can develop.

**What do I mean? Let me explain.**

A false belief is described as an illusion, delusion, misperception, or even a self-fulfilling prophecy.

We often filter experiences through the lens of pain and trauma, causing a belief—whether true or not—to manifest. This often begins in childhood as we develop ideas of what and why something happens to us. If we experienced bullying or abuse as a child, it usually causes us to believe all kinds of lies about our value. Later in life, we may encounter a person who responds to us in a comparable way, says something to us, or even looks like the person who hurt us—and BAM! We are right back in that childhood moment, feeling all the emotions that we felt in that old experience. We feel scared, invaluable, humiliated, or ashamed. What often happens is, in that moment of being triggered, we respond to this person—who has nothing to do with that original pain-point—as if they did. Why? Because we are right back to that moment when we were hurt, and our emotions are stored at a cellular level in our bodies, creating a reaction from a past experience. This is what I mean by a false perception! Triggers are incredible because they can quickly take us from zero to one hundred, transporting us to a different place and time, causing us to react in a way that has nothing to do with the here and now—or the person in the present moment—but causes us to manifest as if it did.

Another way false perceptions can hurt relationships is simply by seeing things from a place of personal insecurity. Again, this stems from a belief system about oneself that does not align with the Word of God. If you believe, for example, you are (FILL IN THE BLANK)—ugly, boring, clumsy, fat, stupid, rejected, unwanted, left out—then that belief will cause you to respond out of that lie. So, if you feel rejected, you may think someone is always talking about you and that nobody likes you. If you were always the last one chosen for your school team, you may perceive that you are unwanted or not good enough. If you were told growing up by a parent that you were a little piggy because you ate a lot, you may always struggle with thinking you are fat—or it becomes a self-fulfilling prophecy because of the stronghold in your mind that holds you as a prisoner to the lie.

Another scenario of unhealthy overindulgence in food can take effect when a person may have experienced love through eating. Suppose the only person you really felt loved by was your adorable, sweet grandma, and every time you visited her, she cooked you a big, delicious meal. Now, you subconsciously equate love with food because of its comforting effect. Or another scenario could be that you were never allowed to have a voice where you could express your thoughts or feelings. That restriction could cause you to either dominate conversations or, conversely, retreat from social situations.

Do you see how powerful our memory bank is? The problem is how false perceptions can stem from how we stored that information yet have no bearing on the actual truth of what is going on in our present moment.

Now, let's say that parent never said "piggy" as a derogatory statement but thought it was cute and endearing. But what happened? That now-grown adult PERCEIVED it very differently as a child, and it affects their life all these years later.

Then we have those people in our lives who have the need to always be right—even if they do not know what they are talking about. Or they do, but just cannot read the room and offer up what has not been invited. We all know someone who is an expert in everything, yet knows nothing—or only knows what their social media influencers have convinced them of, right? This response usually stems from a place of control because they did not have control over their circumstances when they were young. So, they feel like they must take charge of the narrative and lack the discipline of listening to or learning another's ideas.

There are many ways control manifests, but control is always a challenging behavior, whether in personal or business relationships. The root of witchcraft is the fleshly desire to control, dominate, or manipulate, and it stems from insecurity. So, what do you do with triggers, perceptions, or irritations of the flesh?

Years ago, I was taught by a pastor in my life—someone I mentored under—to 'make someone right before you make them wrong.' That was such a powerful teaching moment, and it has never left me. So, when I feel like I am believing the absolute worst about someone or something, I try to make them right first.

How do I do this? I take the belief I am holding onto and hold it against the Word of God—does it align? I say the things I know to be true about the person or situation. For example, I know this person loves me. I know this person would never intentionally hurt me. I know this person is going through a tough time right now. I know this person has yet to surrender xyz in this area of their life. This diffuses the offense.

I also take my feelings, offense, or irritation about someone, and I ask Holy Spirit what it is about me that struggles with this person. Be mindful: not all of our responses are triggers from the past but can be our own character flaws. What is going on inside of me that wants to respond harshly? What caused me to be "rubbed the wrong way" by this person? It is entirely possible that God anoints people to push our buttons to reveal hidden issues in our own hearts. Ask me how I know!

*"God, I invite Your searching gaze into my heart. Examine me through and through; find out everything that may be hidden within me. Put me to the test and sift through all my anxious cares. See if there is any path of pain I'm walking on, and lead me back to Your glorious, everlasting way—the path that brings me back to You."*
**—Psalms 139:23 TPT**

I then walk out the truth of what I know about myself and the other person by humbly checking my own heart. This can be challenging, especially when we want to believe that we are right and have no responsibility in the difficulty of the relationship. I repent for my attitude and any offense I've taken on, surrendering it to God.

Now, victors of trauma often experience lies about themselves, including beliefs of shame. They will need to apply the same strategies, but in relation to what is true about themselves. For example, they will need to choose to speak truth over themselves, such as: *I am deeply loved by God. I am acceptable in Christ. I am worthy of blessing. I was a child – it was not my fault. There is no condemnation in Christ Jesus. Shame is a liar.* Professing and decreeing truth over our lives is an important part of renewing our minds and walking out our healing and deliverance.

*"He heals the wounds of every shattered heart."*
—**Psalm 147:3 TPT**

Let me share a personal story that happened to me many years ago. Around six years into my marriage, I had an experience that led to a false perception. My husband walked in from work one evening and began greeting the kids— all four of them. He asked about their day and discussed whatever came up (nothing unusual—this was normal for him). But something happened in that incident that caused a response of anger in me. I became so upset with him! Seriously, it felt like we'd gotten into a huge argument, or he'd done something grievous to offend me, but he had not. Mind you, all that had happened was what I just described, and it all took place in just a few minutes.

These few minutes took me from 0 to 60 with anger, tears, and nothing short of throwing him into the "doghouse." My emotions were so powerful in that moment! I sobbed in the bathroom, asking God what was going on with me. Why was I so angry? I did not understand my reaction, but I did recognize that it did not fit the offense. My reaction was not justifiable by any sense of the word. So, I called a close prayer friend—someone I trusted, who I knew would pray with me through this. I said, "Something is triggering me, and I don't know what it is, but I need your help praying with me to get to the bottom of what's going on inside of me and uncover whatever lie I'm believing."

Shortly after, she picked me up, and we went to a park and sat in the car, praying. We asked Holy Spirit for direction and to expose the lie I was believing and replace it with His truth. Low and behold, He took me to a memory that was so unexpected. Out of the blue, I saw myself in the home I grew up in, around the age of twelve. I saw myself walking through the front door with my friend. As we entered, my stepfather was sitting in his recliner. He never said hi. He never asked how my day was. He didn't even look our way—no acknowledgment whatsoever! My friend whispered to me, "Is he mad?" I laughed and said, "Oh no, that's how he always is."

And although that was true, and despite my laugh and trying to justify this experience as normal, I felt embarrassed and unseen. What I didn't realize was that this experience—walking into my house that afternoon—marked me. So, I dug deeper and asked

Holy Spirit what it was about this "memory," buried in my subconscious mind, that caused me to be so angry with my husband. Instantly, I was given a word-picture from the Lord. I saw a big rubber stamp with the word "APPROVED" across it—like a stamp used on envelopes at the post office. Then I saw the Lord's hand take this big red stamp and stamp me. I heard Jesus say, "You are approved by Me!"

See, I had been believing something internally—something deep in my cellular memory—that said I was not worthy to be greeted. My day, my struggles, my victories—they didn't matter. Why? Because I was never greeted or asked about my day. Crazy, huh? I had never thought about that situation from decades ago until that moment with the Lord. I had no conscious memory of that day. And yet, that seemingly insignificant moment of walking into my house laid a deep belief barrier in my heart—a lie that caused me to react the way I did with my husband. I had believed that I wasn't important enough to be greeted, and therefore I must not matter to my husband.

Jesus healed me in that moment of seeking His counsel. I have never experienced that trigger again.

*"Go back and tell Hezekiah, the ruler of my people,*
*'This is what the Lord, the God of your father David,*

*says: I have heard your prayer and seen your tears; I will heal you."*
— **2 Kings 20:5 NIV**

I want my dear readers to know that my stepfather is a good man. He was often emotionally detached but never harmed me and was a good provider. At times, he was incredibly supportive—more so than even my mother. He was my roller coaster buddy at amusement parks, and he always celebrated my good report cards. My biological father, due to divorce and the distance of thousands of miles, wasn't a present figure in my life, so my stepfather was the only father role I had. I wish there had been more emotional expression and connection because a child (both boys and girls) needs that from a loving father figure to bring stability and balance to their life. Without a healthy, loving, and involved father figure, a child never understands their value and worth, and they often seek that affirmation from other sources—like I did, ending up as a pregnant teenager.

Even so, during that life-changing teen moment, my stepfather was the supportive and encouraging voice, reassuring me that everything would be okay and we'd get through it together.

My stepfather's lack of engagement wasn't an isolated experience. I saw him respond this way in most of his relationships. He wasn't expressive, talkative, or engaging. He seemed unhappy or unfulfilled in much of his life. Years later, when I was a young adult, one of his brothers casually mentioned how funny my stepfather had been when they were kids—always joking around or pulling pranks. I thought, *What? How did he get so lucky?!* I wondered what stole his joy and caused him to seem so disengaged later in life. I regret never seeing that funny side of him—life would have been so much more enjoyable with more laughter in our home – even a prank or two wouldn't have hurt. But we all have areas to grow in and heal from. Not one person is an exception to this.

I want to give honor to my stepfather for stepping into the role of dad long before he needed to. Being a stepparent was not common in the 1970s, and he stepped into unfamiliar territory and did the best he knew how to do.

I share this story as an example of healing and what Jesus will do when we seek Him with lies that trigger us—especially the ones that seem so irrelevant. His truth brings freedom. Allow these nuggets of wisdom to saturate your heart, and be vulnerable in approaching the Throne of Grace with your own triggers, so you can receive deep healing—even to the very core of every cell in your body.

The Lord is so good! Healing is our bread. We must desire healing and growth, and sometimes, though not always, be willing to go to uncomfortable places before we can be delivered. No matter the situation—the amount of pain or shame buried deep—no matter how insignificant it may seem, the TRUTH really will set you free.

I encourage you to allow yourself the space and freedom to explore triggers with the Holy Spirit. Sit with Him and ask Him to show you every lie, then usher in and replace it with His truth. If you are afraid or have walls difficult to break through, find a pastor or someone with wise, godly counsel rooted in the Word of God and in relationship with the Holy Spirit. They can help facilitate this process with you, praying through the journey—whether it's quick or a long, untangling process of deeply embedded lies. But process is okay! I promise you, the freedom that comes is worth it. We will continually grow and heal as we grow in the fullness of Christ. It only requires humility and a desire to be free. Just say yes!

Lord Jesus, thank you for my friend reading this book and choosing personal and spiritual growth. I pray that they marinate in your presence, submitting their healing to You, so they can blossom and bear much fruit for the kingdom of heaven and leave a restorative healing legacy over their family.

**STEPS TO SOUL HEALING:**

- Find a quiet space with no distractions or interruptions.
- **Pray:** Father God, I submit my healing to You. I lay myself down and choose to yield to Your process of healing and deliverance. I invite the Holy Spirit to expose the lies that I believe and have held onto. Expose the false perceptions (feelings) and belief systems that have had me bound and stuck.
- Think of a recent trigger or memory that caused you discomfort. Do not be fearful. When you ask your Heavenly Father for bread, would He give you a stone? No, but He gives good gifts to those who ask Him. And healing, my friend, is a good, good gift.
- Now wait and see what He brings to your mind. This may be a memory, a word, a scripture, a vision, a picture, or simply a feeling—whatever method He chooses, go with it. Write it down.
- Now ask the Holy Spirit to expose the lie you have believed that is attached to this memory or feeling. Write it down.

- Now ask the Holy Spirit to reveal His truth to replace the lie. Write down what He shows or speaks to your heart.
- Give thanks! Thank the Holy Spirit for facilitating your healing and welcome Him to bring you through more as things surface down the road.

**Note:** As mentioned above, in some cases, finding a Christian counselor or even a trusted friend or pastor—someone rooted in Truth and godly wisdom—may be the best option for your circumstance.

Welcome to being on the other side of that lie. Truth, the very essence of God Himself, is truly an amazing thing. Once you receive THE Truth, the light of God dispels the darkness that kept you shrouded in lies and dysfunctional cycles. It is not complicated; it just takes a willing heart—a heart that chooses freedom over the idols of this world that we turn to, which falsely numb and distract us from the healing of God. When you get into the habit of surrender and allow God to do what He does best—bring lasting transformation—healing will be something you embrace and run to, rather than deny or hide from. It is a non-negotiable in the life of a Believer. God has a perfect path for you that requires your willingness to allow His healing to complete its work. His desire is for a healed Bride that can walk in fruitfulness and maturity. The gentleness of God in this process is profound. He will take us step by step, a little here, a little there, and bring us through as victors on the other side of healing. But the choice is always ours. He will not force Himself on us but waits for our "yes." Friend, give Him your "yes." It will be the best "yes" to walking out your abundance on this earth and glorifying the name of Jesus.

# CHAPTER EIGHT

## Your Portion: Yoke Destroyer

*"For freedom Christ has set us free; stand firm therefore, and do not submit again to a yoke of slavery."*
— **Galatians 5:1 ESV**

When it comes to healing, we cannot ignore the importance of deliverance. It goes hand in hand with healing. Too often, the very word *deliverance* creates all kinds of responses from both believers and unbelievers alike. Some find the word itself frightening, while others have been taught that it is only for the unsaved. But I am here to say that is not true. Deliverance and healing are the children's bread. That means it's for the believer.

The Greek word for "demon-possessed" does not mean ownership of your body but that someone is being demonized, tormented, or coming under the power of a demon. Many ask, "How in the world can God live in me and a demon?" You are a spirit! You live in a body, and you have a soul. Your spirit cannot be demon-possessed, and a demon cannot enter into your spirit. The place they attach to is your soul and your body. Your soul is the seat of your mind, will, and emotions. Demons seek to invade the hearts of the redeemed through these avenues, and if Satan can stop you from claiming your inheritance, he will. So no, a demon cannot take full possession of a born-again believer, but they can certainly bring oppression, depression, and sickness upon your soul and physical body. Regardless of how they enter, if they are there, you want them gone!

*Jesus responded, "It's not right for a man to take bread from his children and throw it to the dogs."*
*"You're right, Lord," she replied.*
*"But even the puppies get to eat the crumbs that fall from the prince's table."*
*Then Jesus answered her, "Dear woman, your faith is strong! What you desire will be done for you." And at that very moment, her daughter was instantly set free from demonic torment.*
**—Matthew 15:26-28 TPT**

Have you ever considered the subject of "deliverance" in the Bible? Have you given it much thought? What was your first reaction? What is your belief today? Perhaps you were taught in church, or through Hollywood, that deliverance is only for the possessed or wickedly evil person. We have all experienced, at one time or another, different feelings on the topic—often out of ignorance. I want to help you understand

God's word about deliverance and to help remove any hindrances to your receiving all the liberty God has for you.

Jesus came to destroy every yoke or bondage the devil has placed on God's children. In Isaiah 10, we read that it's the anointing that does the destroying. What is the anointing? It's the Spirit of the Lord. A "yoke" in Hebrew refers to a wooden bar or frame by which two animals, such as oxen, are joined at the necks to work together. It symbolizes subjugation (control), burden, or servitude. It can also represent any form of oppression or heavy burden placed upon individuals or nations. A yoke could represent the burden of slavery or domination, as well as the covenantal relationship with God, who offers a yoke that is easy and a burden that is light. —**Matthew 11:29-30**

*"Could it be any clearer that our former identity is now and forever deprived of its power? For we were co-crucified with him to dismantle the stronghold of sin within us, so that we would not continue to live one moment longer submitted to sin's power."*
**—Romans 6:6**

Since the Bible says we all sin and fall short, this is not referring to all sin but to habitual or intentional sin in the lives of those who belong to Jesus. Jesus came to overcome sin and destroy the devil's work. Look around, and you'll see born-again believers bound by all sorts of things, caught in cycles of dysfunction and sin. We have churches filled with people who are desperately seeking freedom, yet many times, they leave a service with nothing more than a neatly packaged program that satisfies their senses but leaves them void of true heart change.

The first thing people need to know is that needing deliverance is nothing to be ashamed of. That is exactly what the devil wants—to make you feel embarrassed to step out and say, "Help me!" Do not allow pride to keep you bound from abundant life. We are to confess our sins to one another that we may be healed. Confession and repentance go together. I have seen people confess all day long but have no genuine heart repentance, grieving the Spirit of the Lord, and therefore nothing changes. We need to be a people quick to renounce our sin, the participation in wickedness, and shameful acts done in secret—even generational sin that has transcended into our family line. Let me say it again, deliverance is not a terrible thing! Some would rather sit in their pride, remain bound, and repeat cycles of sin than admit they need deliverance.

To renounce is a powerful declaration to heaven and earth. It is a formal announcement that signifies you are giving up or declaring you will no longer adhere to a belief or position, or reject and relinquish something you will no longer engage in or use. It is a public profession that you no longer own, support, or will be connected to something you were once a part of, or that a demonic door was opened to over your life—either by you or your ancestors. There are also doors that can be opened in your life by another person, through no fault of your own. This can happen through abuse, pornography introduced by a friend, a child innocently seeing something on the internet, or because a parent buys illicit content on their television. Whatever the means, the enemy can legally enter your life and take up residence in your home, even affecting your children and generations to come.

*"Therefore say to the people of Israel, 'This is what the Sovereign Lord says: Repent! Turn from your idols and renounce all your detestable practices!'"*
**—Ezekiel 14:6 NIV**

By renouncing your involvement or participation in a detestable practice, you break a demonic covenant and stronghold over your life or family line because it sends a notice of eviction to the enemy. Your words have the power to bring life or death. To renounce out loud serves the devil notice, making a decree against him to refuse to acknowledge anything that once belonged to him through the legal door of entry. If you have something to renounce, say so! Whatever the Holy Spirit leads you to renounce, needs to be renounced—and it can be anything from lust, pornography, jealousy, pride, hate, vanity, gluttony, occult practices, religion, fear, suicide, abuse, addictions, greed...you get the picture.

It is also important to have understanding of what deliverance could look like. If you understand these things, it will help prevent fear and allow you to recognize what is happening in yourself or another person without passing judgment. This is crucial because we are entering a season of great deliverance for the followers of Christ, and a revival upon the earth like never before, as Jesus prepares His bride for His return. So, what can deliverance look like? It can manifest through crying, shrieking, vomiting, bodily contorting, coughing, or even yawning. Sometimes, there is no apparent physical reaction, but freedom is experienced nonetheless. Again, do not be afraid! It is Jesus' anointing that breaks this bondage and sets the captives free. Instead, rejoice.

As I close, it is important to recognize that deliverance is often the easy part. We can see people set free by the Spirit of the Lord, but they can still fall back into sin patterns. This is because deliverance needs to be followed by discipleship. You need a spiritual father or mother, or a mentor, to walk beside you and help you grow in the things of God. Someone who can speak into your life and hold you accountable to the Word of God. Someone you give permission to walk alongside you—someone you are willing to be teachable with, even when it hurts. I read an insert in my journal from a teaching by Apostle Arayomi that said, "To go from deliverance to dominion, you must embrace discipleship! God's gift of freedom comes through confessing sins and recognizing the spiritual roots of your problems."

The importance of discipleship cannot be underestimated; it is key to walking in the freedom you have been given. You must be willing to submit to accountability and mentorship, to grow and learn while establishing a firm foundation as you discover how to implement the Word and boundaries in your everyday life. To not do so is foolish and will often result in continued cycles of defeat and past sin patterns.

I have watched people who choose to do it alone or convince themselves that they do not need accountability fall hard. This usually happens due to pride and the fear of being vulnerable in their growth process. The lie the devil whispers in their ear is, "You got this!" And so, the beginning of deception takes hold, and the chains of darkness enshroud them once again, keeping them in shame while hiding in the dark. The only way out is to expose what is in the dark to the light. This is carried out through daily surrender to Christ and ongoing discipleship with a mature Christian, rooted in prayer and the Word of God. It is someone you will allow to speak into your life—even when it hurts. You might be thinking, "Well, I hear my pastor every Sunday." That's good, but not enough when you are struggling with bondage. You must have someone personally come alongside you, to encourage you, hold you to biblical truth, and keep you accountable as you build a sturdy foundation. This is the only way to grow into the person you were created to be. The choice is yours. Choose wisely. You are worth it! A life of love, joy, peace, and abundance depends on it.

*"Where there is no guidance, a people falls, but in an abundance of counselors, there is safety."*
**—Proverbs 11:14 ESV**

# CHAPTER NINE

## Family Renewal: Betrayal And Boundaries

*"For a son dishonors his father, a daughter rises up against her mother, a daughter-in-law against her mother-in-law—a man's enemies are the members of his own household."*
—**Micah 7:6 NIV**

Have you ever wondered why there is so much family division? If you're alive on this planet, chances are high that you've experienced hurt or some form of betrayal from people you love.

Research on families that experience infighting reveals a complex interplay of trust, emotional dynamics, and outside influences. Betrayal within families—such as infidelity, emotional manipulation, or trust violations—often results in significant emotional distress and fractured relationships. All of these can trigger feelings of anger, sadness, and mistrust, which hinder communication and strain family bonds. Poorly managed conflicts—whether between spouses, siblings, co-parents, or parents and adult children—can escalate from everyday disputes to more entrenched divisions.

Micah, in the Scripture above, gives us a heads-up and highlights the gravity of the moral and spiritual decay that can affect a household. The act of dishonoring one's father would have been seen as a severe breach of social and religious duty, showing a breakdown of family structure. The verb in Hebrew for a daughter who "rises" against her mother is *qum*, meaning "to stand up," "establish," or "rise against," suggesting active rebellion or confrontation. The relationship between a daughter-in-law and her mother-in-law in ancient times, as it is today, often involves issues of loyalty and family integration. The reference to a man's enemies being in his own household—traditionally a place of safety and unity—captures the tragic irony of internal strife, where those who should be closest and most supportive become adversaries. This reflects the prophetic theme of judgment and the consequences of turning away from God's covenant, as internal divisions mirror the spiritual and moral failings of a nation. These phrases suggest a breakdown in the family unit, which is crucial for the health and prosperity of the household.

I wasn't sure whether to include this chapter because family conflict is so prolific in society and requires much more than what can fit into a single chapter. However, since it has been a significant and difficult part of my own story of surrender and dying to self while trusting God, I felt it was important to share. I've learned that carrying my cross when it comes to the hurt of loved ones takes you to a whole new level of dependence and trust in God. At times, it feels like the final nail in the coffin. If you can learn and grow through this life lesson, then nothing else the enemy has will faze you. No other rejection you will face in your calling and purpose will sting as badly or knock you off your Jesus-focus. If you walk through rejection or betrayal from those closest to you and still choose forgiveness and love, then nothing else pales in comparison. Jesus is magnified and receives all the glory. Well done, good and faithful servant.

The number of tears and weight of grief experienced when those who mean the most to you hurt you can be devastating. When betrayal is encountered by a spouse, a parent, or even a child—nothing seems to cut so deeply. What you must do is learn to intercept the thoughts that lead you down rabbit trails in your mind, because they serve no purpose but to cause misery. It's a dark place that can bury you in a hole, keeping you stuck and smothered by lies that make it hard to breathe. I've experienced seasons of betrayal that are mind-boggling. Never in 100 years would I have thought family members would choose to cause such wounding. Then, more thoughts creep in as I try to make sense of it—asking, "What could I have possibly done so terribly that justifies this kind of pain?" Oh, those vain imaginations that bombard our minds—conversations with ourselves that rob us of time and sleep. On top of that, the sadness can overwhelm you when you think of all the memories being forfeited. Months and years pass. I saw a picture of a vacation I wasn't included in. Left out. Forgotten. Unloved. Unwanted. These words swirled through my mind.

Divisions in a family do so much damage! People can become so caught up in their own justification and reasoning for their bitterness and hate—pride, really—that they have no idea how their actions leave a violent tornado trail of broken hearts. It can be far-reaching, leaving behind debris that can take years to clean up. Usually, sides are taken, or children or grandchildren are used as pawns in a series of manipulation tactics to "get even." If this is you, please stop! It is wicked and not in line with Kingdom living. Often, the aftereffects end up hurting the most innocent, as they are the ones who feel the aftershock of a family unwilling to yield with humility, allowing a stronghold of bitterness to destroy family unity and legacy.

*"A thief has only one thing in mind—he wants to steal, slaughter, and destroy. But I have come to give you everything in abundance, more than you expect—*

*life in its fullness until you overflow. "*
**—John 10:10 TPT**

I will share two personal stories related to family that I've walked through—one with extended family that has lasted over seventeen years, and another for about four years with an immediate family member. The one with extended family was about me including someone at our Christmas gathering, which was held at my home that year. The person I had invited was also part of my family and had nowhere else to go. Surely, everyone could extend grace for this one-time event. However, two people upset about this decided to simply be no-shows on Christmas Day. No call, no attempt to share their feelings or discuss the matter— just empty seats at the table that holiday. A few weeks later, I was able to express my disappointment and hurt over the lack of love and respect for me, and their unwillingness to make a phone call to tell me they wouldn't be there.

I've always been one to speak what's on my heart and not push things under the rug, which sadly many people prefer. The inability to communicate is staggering in many households. I'm a very honest communicator—some would say to a fault, especially with those who dodge confrontation. This set in motion years of separation, as the person I expressed my hurt to became defensive and refused to take responsibility for the hurt their actions caused, or even acknowledge my heart or try to understand the predicament their requests would have put me in. I spent the first few years reaching out periodically with cards or invitations for coffee and talks, but to no avail. Mind you, this wasn't some distant relative but someone I loved and was close to—a person with whom I had never experienced turmoil before. But through much prayer and the feelings of more rejection that surfaced from many failed attempts to reconnect, I felt peace to let it go and give it to God. I walked away. I never expected something so trivial, at least in the grand scale of life issues, to cause so much heartache. But that is what pride does, doesn't it? It twists and pulls people under while convincing them that they are right, no matter the cost. Pride is a great destroyer! It will swiftly dismantle marriages, families, and friendships without a wince. God hates pride! It is the very thing that got Lucifer cast out of heaven and separated from God forever.

*"These six things the LORD hates; indeed, seven are repulsive to Him: A proud look [the attitude that makes one overestimate oneself and discount others], a lying tongue, and hands that shed innocent blood, a heart that creates wicked plans, feet that run swiftly to evil, a false witness who breathes out lies [even*

*half-truths], and one who spreads discord among brothers.*"
**—Proverbs 6:16-19 AMP**

Pride is a despicable act and something every person will struggle with at some point in life. The Bible says pride goes before destruction, and haughtiness before a fall. That means the harder you lift yourself up in pride, the harder you will fall in disgrace. Part of maturing in Christ is learning to grow in humility, which captures the affection of the Lord. You need to understand that the power to destroy everything in its path comes from pride. Rebellion is as sinful as witchcraft, and stubbornness is as bad as worshiping idols. So, if you're one who makes excuses for your stubbornness and refuses to repent, know that demons are attached to it. It requires true humbling and renouncing to break free from this powerful beast.

*"But I have more to say about Leviathan, the sea beast, his enormous bulk, his beautiful shape. Who would even dream of piercing that tough skin or putting those jaws into bit and bridle? And who would dare knock at the door of his mouth, filled with row upon row of fierce teeth? His pride is invincible; nothing can make a dent in that pride. Nothing can get through that proud skin—impervious to weapons and weather, the thickest and toughest hides,*

*impenetrable!"*
**—Job 42:12-17 MSG**

The willingness and humility needed to talk out hard things, to hear someone who disagrees with you, and to put love above everything else, can be lost in the fog of self-righteousness. Sadly, families need to learn better communication skills and how to live authentically with one another—truly doing life together. Choosing to love and hear each other, rather than living in offense, is the honorable thing to do. No matter how hard one might try to water down the Word of God, it is crystal clear in *Matthew 6* that if we do not forgive others their sins, our Father will not forgive ours. There is no way around this, and it will require genuine humility to extend to another—especially if they have hurt you. But by His grace, it is possible. It is not always a feeling, but an act of obedience to the one who gave His life for us even when we were yet sinners. How can we withhold from another what was so freely given to us?

Forgiveness is necessary if you are a true believer, even if it is not reciprocated. But relationship, however, requires two people—and it is not one-sided. You cannot force what the other refuses. But you can make your peace, extend love, and leave the outcome to the Lord. Learn to be okay with families that do not respond in kind. They may not extend dinner invitations or go out of their way to stay connected. Love them anyway. They may be busy, they may not enjoy your company, or they may not feel comfortable with the Jesus you carry in your heart. It's okay. Love them and pray for them anyway. If relational distress is provoked by the enemy, trust God for the healing and restoration of it. And if it's God allowing the separation, it may be because they are not meant to go where you are going in this season. Rest in Him.

Do you remember the television series *Parenthood*? Oh my gosh, my husband and I loved watching that show! The series was about the Braverman family, consisting of the retired parents, four adult children and their spouses, and the grandkids. The show focused on how each family faced challenges together. The family could choose to deal with those obstacles through support and love, or allow the circumstances to tear them apart. In the end, they always chose love. After each show aired, my husband and I would look at each other and say with an emphatic, earnest voice, "I want to be a Braverman!" The show got it right because, in the end, no matter how hard a relationship dynamic was, love always won. To step into healthy communication, a family must be willing to hear and respect each other, even when they disagree. There's nothing wrong with honest conflict; it's better than dishonest harmony. And secondly, choosing love over being right should be our goal. Let me be clear— healthy boundaries are necessary in dysfunctional or toxic family settings, but honoring one another is pivotal. If more families heard the words "I love you" and "I value you," it would be a game-changer for many homes.

The second situation I've walked through involves a close family member and is much more complicated because it includes a grandchild—one I had a deeply special bond with, much like the one my brother and I had with our grandparents. That kind of relationship is a precious gift. It's one that offers love, protection, and a sense of safety, especially during difficult times like my parents' divorce. If you've never experienced a grandparent's adoration, I am truly sorry. There's nothing quite like it.

This bond with my grandchild developed through difficult circumstances in their life. Without going into too much detail, challenges arose almost immediately after one of our children remarried. Yet, I could see the warning signs a year before the shift occurred. There was a dramatic change in the hearts of both parties— an effort to divide where there was once unity. The pain of this assault on our family took me completely by surprise, nearly knocking me out of commission. It was the hardest loss I've faced, a cross like no other. Trusting Jesus with this was incredibly difficult, especially after years of waiting for Him to restore the first broken family fraction. The thought of going through a similar waiting period frightened me.

I knew in my spirit that this was a battle I couldn't fight on my own; only the Holy Spirit could break through the pride and delusion surrounding this situation. As I poured out my heart to Jesus in prayer and journaling, He comforted me with reminders of His love. I could feel His presence, reassuring me with whispers of, "It's going to be okay." As I looked to Him, His truth exposed the lies and grounded me in His promises.

If you're facing betrayal, I urge you to look to Him. The alternative—anger and bitterness—will poison your heart. Jesus warns us in **Luke 17** that offenses will come, but "woe" to those through whom they come. The dictionary defines "woe" as affliction, agony, anguish, and misery. I'd rather grow in learning how not to be offended.

Betrayal isn't about the one who's hurt, but about something deeper going on in the heart of the one inflicting pain. How others treat you reflects them; how you react reflects you. For the betrayer, it's a chance to uncover the true state of their heart, and for the betrayed, it's an opportunity for healing and resurrection. This process may be difficult, but it's in the death of something precious that new growth and faith are born.

In your family dynamics, remember that there will be times when people will blame you just to avoid feeling guilty for what they've done. They don't want to take responsibility. You must let go of the pain, forgive, and move on. You may face slander, lies, or stories that serve someone else's agenda. Let it go. Don't feel the need to defend yourself. Jesus lived without a reputation, and we too should be okay with others not knowing our side of the story. The ones who are speaking the loudest are often the ones whose actions should give us pause. Trust God's vindication, and keep your peace focused on doing His will. Sometimes, this is the most misunderstood power move you can make.

If you find yourself in family pain, ask yourself: Do you identify more with Jesus or your offender? Betrayal has a way of exposing your heart's true identity. If you don't know who you are in Christ, you won't be able to carry the glory He has for you.

Sometimes, God allows separation from loved ones as part of your refining process, preparing you for your calling. The experience of being removed from someone's life can feel undeniably cruel at the time.

But as you press into the Lord and put your hope in Him, you will learn to rest in the assurance that, somehow, in the grand design of your story, it is part of His plan. God's protection will cover you as you walk through it and rise above.

Human effort cannot always explain the "why" in these situations, and words often fail to express the depth of grief that comes with them. Some people are simply not meant to go where you are destined to go. Because of this, your refining process may require separate roads from those you love, even if only for a season.

Your God-given authority is not to bow to the masters of control and manipulation—forces that are sadly prevalent in family divisions, especially when children are involved—but to rise above and lay His plumb line of righteousness. It is of no benefit to play into someone's victimhood when they are suffering the consequences of their own choices. You have permission to distance yourself from those who act like victims in situations they created.

God sees all, knows all, and one day, everything will be revealed. While we wait for the Vindicator of the injustices we face, remember that *Jesus is a Restoring God*, and His heart is for family—your family! If you are in the trenches of family brokenness, trust the work

He is doing through one of the hardest trials you can endure. Carry your cross as you walk this journey of surrender.

At the time of writing this, I am still waiting for Jesus' restoration over these family divisions. If you are in a similar place, know that death is only half the story. Do not be afraid to die to what you love. I won't lie—it will be hard. It will bring rivers of tears and what seems like insurmountable heartbreak. It is terrifying not knowing how long you will have to walk this out.

But the good news? The other half of the story is resurrection, and it lies on the other side of your sacrifice. His promises are true, so decree the *yes and amen* over your family and loved ones.

*"I've come to start a fire on this earth—how I wish it were blazing right now! I've come to change everything, turn everything rightside up—how I long for it to be finished! Do you think I came to smooth things over and make everything nice? Not so. I've come to disrupt and confront! From now on, when you find five in a house, it will be—*
*Three against two, and two against three;*
*Father against son, and son against father;*
*Mother against daughter, and daughter against mother; Mother-in-law against bride, and bride*

*against mother-in-law."*
—**Luke 12:49-53 MSG**

This passage describes how Jesus came not to bring peace, but division. For a long time, this Scripture puzzled me—especially since family is God's idea. Why would He allow division?

I believe it is to expose false peace in our hearts, a peace that can only be revealed when factions arise in our households. True peace comes through a right relationship with God. Even if we grow up in Christ-centered homes—which I did not—we cannot fully know this peace that surpasses all understanding until we encounter difficulties and offenses that sift our hearts. Only then do we realize that what comes out of our mouths in these disruptive family dynamics is often an overflow of the darkness hidden in our own hearts.

Family division can uncover wounds, false expectations, and lies we have believed about one another. Often, the painful and explosive outbursts that follow do nothing but leave us questioning our worth in our own families. Yet, in this brokenness, we arrive at a critical intersection—the moment we recognize our need for true reconciliation, the kind that fosters love and healing.

This is also the cost of following Jesus. Not everyone in a family chooses to surrender to Him, and where the flesh reigns, division will follow. Our task is to obey God, trusting His plan through all seasons of faith, knowing that *Jesus is the restorer of brokenness.*

Healing is possible, but it requires forgiveness. Forgiveness is releasing the right to hurt someone in return. This does not mean God's justice is forgotten—that is for Him to handle. When you surrender to God, He will enlarge your capacity to love and forgive, even those who never apologize.

The Bible is full of examples we can learn from. One of Jesus' closest friends betrayed Him. Those closest to David betrayed him. Joseph's own family betrayed him. Loving our enemies—including those in our own households—is not something we can do in our own strength. It can only happen when we die to ourselves so that Christ can love through us.

There are two great paths to genuine spiritual growth—great love and great suffering. Loving those who betray us is graduate-level Kingdom living, and it is only possible through Christ's love flowing through us.

As I close, I want to leave you with this: hurt people will hurt people. The enemy is a master at division, which is his modus operandi; always seeking to wreak havoc in a family to cause separation – because a house divided cannot stand and he will use whatever brokenness in another persons life to try and bring it down. Let God begin the work in your own heart so that you can cast love instead of stones. It's impossible to please God without faith, and there's no greater display of faith than in the darkest, most painful areas of our lives. God may ask you to let go of people, not just the bad, but the good too. Grieve it, let go, and trust Him. He is a good Father who will save, heal, and restore all that is meant to be. See it, speak it, and believe it.

# CHAPTER TEN

## Breaking Barriers: You Can Do This!

*"The breaker [the Messiah, who opens the way] shall go up before them [liberating them]. They will break out, pass through the gate and go out; So their King goes on before them, The LORD at their head."*
—**Micah 2:13 AMP**

Through the many chapters you have now read and, hopefully, gleaned from, the question of why you experience difficult things in your life should at least be starting to make sense. The Word of God is a refuge for us, and His Holy Spirit is a great Comforter in our journey on this earth. Trials are hard and confusing at times, but they are not in vain. It may feel like they are unrelenting and hard on the heels of one another—blasting you before you can catch your breath. They may even cause you to question your faith or wonder if God has somehow forgotten you in the vast pool of humanity. You may even find yourself ready to toss in the game towel and call it quits. Trials and testing are hard! They press us on every side, squeezing us—crushing us—leaving what seems like nothing more than a dried raisin. But that is the point. That is the process of refining; the process of carrying our cross and dying to self. God loves you so much that He promises to complete the work He has begun in you. He takes you from glory to glory, and in the process, makes a fine vintage from the hard pressing.

*"Friends, when life gets really difficult, don't jump to the conclusion that God isn't on the job. Instead, be glad that you are in the very thick of what Christ experienced. This is a spiritual refining process, with glory just around the corner."*
**—1 Peter 4:12-13 MSG**

As I have said in an earlier chapter, surrender and dying is not a one-and-done deal. It is a lifelong process to build in us His character. There simply is no other way, my friend, but be encouraged, because the Lord Jesus leads us through each circumstance and promises to never forsake us (to give up, to leave, abandon, to quit, to desert, to depart, or withdraw). The Lord does not lie to us. He will be with you every step of the way, and as you yield to Him and allow Him to cultivate the absolute best fruit in your life, you will come out better, stronger, and more resilient than you could ever imagine. As Jesus was perfected through His suffering (Hebrews 2:10), so will we be. The Lord is gentle and allows us only a portion of testing at a time. We may not think so, but He knows what is necessary for the destiny He's prepared for us, and each of us will walk out the trials according to the measure of faith He has given us. Each of us has a different path and calling—the higher the calling, the more intense and confusing the trials.

My journey has been filled with some pretty crazy trials—seriously, trials that hit you from the backside, and you have no idea where they even came from. I've experienced levels of rejection from just about every close family member for no justifiable reason, and I am talking about from the people in my life who really mattered—the ones you count on for love and support—the family God gives us that should be our soft place to fall. I have been hit with job loss and intense financial hardship—and I mean where every door of opportunity shut! Doors not only slammed closed but locked with double bolts! I have experienced prodigal children. I have been lied to and lied about. I have experienced a costly court battle. Even dishonor and hatred from one of the most unexpected sources in my life and a part of my heart. I have learned what being stripped from almost everything feels like and having to put my trust in the only One who could relate to my disappointment, grief, and pain; the only One who promises to restore all that has been lost or stolen; the only One who can redeem the lost time and memories missed.

Through the process of refining, I have learned things I could have never learned any other way. I have learned that each trial was to build in me mountain-moving faith and reliance on my King. I had to resolve within my spirit that God is who He says He is and allow my full surrender to the pain, discomfort, and people's opinions. By no means am I saying this is easy—it is not. It is a process and often takes longer to work out than we would have hoped it would—usually because we want to hold onto the anger as we feel justified in our bitterness. I am here to tell you that belief is a downright lie, and it only leads to bondage in your own life. Forgiveness must be given—it is not an option if you belong to Jesus. Holding onto hate and unforgiveness destroys you, not them, from the inside out, and it will keep you away from the presence of God and prevent you from even hearing Him for your own life. It can also literally manifest in your body at a cellular level, causing sickness and disease.

I am grateful that I have been equipped with the truth that every detail of our lives is woven together to fit into God's perfect plan. God's anointing is what breaks every chain of bondage—and to walk in that anointing and spiritual authority, you must go through cultivation. To be a life builder and bring this anointing and impartation to others, I first had to surrender to the work of His hand. He is the Potter, and

I am the clay. No evil thing comes from Him, but He will use every bit of it, flipping it on its head, if we stand on His Word.

**Jesus is the breaker!** And the anointing that breaks the yoke of slavery or bondage in our life comes through trials. Allow the tests to form a mighty reservoir that will annihilate the works of darkness. Nothing is wasted! Nothing is in vain! Get this revelation deep in your spirit and allow it to transform your thinking so that while you process the trials and pain that come your way, you can have expected hope in knowing God is with you.

*"And it shall come to pass in that day, that his burden shall be taken away from off thy shoulder, and his yoke from off thy neck, and the yoke shall be destroyed because of the anointing."*
**—Isaiah 10:27 KJV**

I want you to know that *you CAN do this!* You were created for this life you've been given! You were created and set apart by God to be here right now, in this time in history, because you have something in you that nobody else has. You are a unique and one-of-a-kind part of the body of Christ that we need. Nobody else has what you have, and what you can impart to the world through your own experiences and testimony.

*You CAN live a holy and righteous life!* You CAN break barriers that have held you down for far too long! Say it with me: "I CAN do this! I CAN break barriers through my surrender." When you grasp this necessary step of surrender, the process quickens.

I wish I had a better understanding when I was younger of the security in carrying my cross and ultimately dying to self. It may seem like an oxymoron, but there is no safer place than being in the process of carrying your cross and choosing to die. God's got you! This is the key to living an amazing Kingdom life—a life that matches nothing else you could possibly create on your own.

As you move forward in your destiny, hand-crafted by God, start seeing yourself right now, busting down the barriers. Every hindrance and obstacle that has side-swiped you is crashing down. Every disappointment is shattered because you now know it is the path least taken—the road less traveled—the dirt-laden mile to the rugged cross. Your King Jesus goes before you and leads the way. You have nothing to fear! Did you hear me? *YOU. HAVE. NOTHING. TO. FEAR.*

Fear is just a mirage that makes you think you see something that you really are not. Its sole purpose is to get your eyes off Jesus, onto yourself, and into your feelings. Your safety is in His presence, and His anointing breaks the yokes off of you.

So go ahead and build that reservoir. Fill it to overflowing with the oil that comes from the trials of your life, then annihilate the works of darkness with it. You were made for such a time as this. Never retreat, mighty warrior—simply reload!

# CHAPTER ELEVEN

## Expansion: God's Plan For You

*"Hear me when I call, O God of my righteousness: Thou hast enlarged me when I was in distress; have mercy upon me, and hear my prayer."*
**—PSALM 4:1 KJV**

Have you ever considered that you can be enlarged by distress? I mean, I have read that Psalm on numerous occasions, and it fell flat. Then, suddenly, after one more read, the lights are turned on. Don't you get absolutely enlivened when that happens — when revelation is illuminated on something that seems so simple and apparently evident, but then hits you right smack in the middle of the forehead? I mean, think about it. Read it again. Wowza! Let's take a quick look at what these two words mean:

**Enlarge:** To make larger in size, to make larger in scope or effect; increase; to become larger; grow or swell. (The American Heritage Dictionary of the English Language, 5th Edition)

**Distress:** Great pain, anxiety, or sorrow; acute physical or mental suffering; affliction; trouble. (dictionary.com)

Have you ever been in a state of distress? A place where you have felt the pressure of pain, disappointment, or delay? Maybe even experiencing anxiety or unrelenting questions of how to overcome so you can have forward movement. I want you to consider, for a moment, the distress you have experienced in the past or find yourself in today in this season of life. What do you do when His promises seem out of reach or you feel forgotten by the lover of your soul? When things He's promised you — things long awaited — have seemingly passed you by?

Even Jesus felt forgotten. Around 3 p.m., the afternoon He hung on the cross, He cried out, "My God, my God, why hast Thou forsaken me?" This was not merely bodily pain but the bitter cry and agony of the soul — an incalculable affliction of soul. There was no one to comfort Him in this heaviness as He took on the sins of the world and the light of God's countenance was temporarily removed from Him. He felt alone; abandoned! He was left to feel the full and crushing weight of sin. Distress would be an understatement for what our Jesus went through for us.

Have you felt abandoned, rejected, or forgotten? How about the excruciating heartache from someone you love? Just the waiting for breakthrough can feel exhausting, can't it? It can even cause us to feel

111

afflicted in our soul with the weight of waiting. Even the Scriptures tell us in **Proverbs 13**, "A hope deferred makes the heart sick, but a desire fulfilled is a tree of life."

Jesus knows what it is like to hunger and thirst, to endure sleepless nights and exhausting days, to experience agonizing pain and betrayal from those closest to Him. And even to pour Himself out to those who are hostile in return for their actions and nasty words. Consider that His cousin was murdered, His family misunderstood Him, His hometown rejected Him, and He watched as His mother's soul was crushed by the loss of her son. People used Him, flattered Him, criticized Him, lied about Him, and abandoned Him. They mocked Him, humiliated Him, whipped Him, and watched Him die an excruciating death.

**THERE IS NO SUFFERING WE CAN EXPERIENCE THAT JESUS CANNOT RELATE TO!** He is acquainted with our pain; with our distress.

*"He understands humanity, for as a Man, our magnificent King-Priest was tempted in every way just as we are, and conquered sin."*
**—Hebrews 5:15 TPT**

I have personally walked through many difficult things in my life — experiencing distress in each one to different degrees. They all were hard. Each circumstance set me up for greater trust in the Lord. Each one caused me to lean in, allowing me the opportunity to die to or hold on to my life as I knew it. Distress that was going to make me or break me. I can look back now and know how my God was in it and stretched me as He enlarged me in every area, but mostly my heart.

At the time of this writing, I have been married for nearly 30 years; a marriage covenant that began by saying yes to God, my husband, and our blended family of four children. If you have experienced the blended family dynamics, it comes with not only the challenges a traditional family experiences but a host of others. Different parenting methods, exes, children adapting to new family dynamics, less alone time at the outset, more expenses in general, but also the likelihood of child support. New blended family marriages are forged in what seems like a hotter fire. Just so much more opportunity for offense and reasons to throw in the towel. In this place of distress, I was enlarged with a greater capacity to love children who were not mine biologically, but who mean the world to me, and I could not imagine life without. By the way, Jesus had a blended family and was likely the man He was on this earth because of the stepfather He had.

Within about five years of being married, I wanted to own my own business. I had hoped for a child with my husband but didn't want to be confined to a 9-to-5 job like I had been as a single mother. I longed for more freedom to be a mother and not have to put my baby in childcare for someone else to raise. While this works for some people, for me, it was always a sadness I carried when I had to do it with my little one.

Long story short, I determined that owning my own business would be my best shot at freedom and the ability to set my own hours. For successful businesses, that's partially true, but there's a lot of hard work involved, too. I purchased a business that ultimately led to us filing for bankruptcy. Within a few short months, we suspected the sellers had defrauded us with their financials. A long, four-year court battle ensued, and because we were subtly manipulated into putting our home as collateral, legal counsel advised us that the only way to protect our home until the courts ruled was to file for bankruptcy, which locked our house from being touched.

It was one of the hardest and most humbling experiences of our lives—a Job season of loss: loss of money, reputation, material things, and pride. This battle was six figures costly and drained us financially, putting a ton of stress on our young marriage. Thankfully, a couple of family members were able to loan us money to help cover court costs during that time. During these rough days, we had a Christmas where we literally had a "Snoopy" tree—a tiny little tree because we simply didn't have money for anything bigger. We even got creative with using every can of food we had in the cabinet, using up just about every can of "something" we had. Hamburger and rice became a staple, not joking! We called it the "poor man's meal."

In the midst of this distress, God enlarged us. He taught us that He's our Provider! He also allowed our family to experience a more powerful Christmas than we had ever had before. As the kids said, it was one of their most memorable, actually having less. We experienced a deeper appreciation for family. There was a lot of stretching during this season. Although it was difficult for both of us, my husband struggled more than I did, often verbalizing that he thought I was crazy as I demonstrated joy and confidence in God's protection. He'd say things like, "Our lives are falling apart, and you're over here acting like it's no big deal!" But I was learning that my words mattered, and my heart needed to align with the Truth. If Jesus promised to never leave me or forsake me, why would I doubt

Him? If He promised to be my Vindicator, why would I panic over something I had no control over?

Jesus enlarged our hearts once again and increased our faith to not lean on our own understanding. He broke the hold that money had over us and caused a generous spirit to rise in me. We did win the court battle for breach of contract and fraud. However, we were not reimbursed for our legal fees. Boy, did that hurt! But God still made a way for us to pay all the debtors from the bankruptcy filing, as well as the family members who had loaned us money. Our credit was destroyed in that season, but our integrity was upheld as we paid everyone we had borrowed from. In the end, Jesus was glorified, and we were enlarged in our distress. A win-win!

Father God is so good! He really is the most trustworthy person you could ever put your faith in. So, when you've begged God to remove your troubles and He denies your desperate request, when you experience tormenting, all-consuming pain with no relief, know that you can share in the fellowship of Jesus' suffering—and as you yield to Him, you will find a precious intimacy that you didn't have before.

There is purpose in our distress, and we grow beyond it. Take a look at these two different translations. I love both as they describe spaciousness and freedom:

*"When hard pressed, I cried to the Lord, and He brought me into a SPACIOUS place."*
**—Psalm 118:5 NIV**

*"In my distress, I prayed to the LORD, and the LORD answered me and set me free."*
**—Psalm 118:5 NLT**

God expands our anointing under pressure! His expansion includes our character development, competence, and maturity. That is some great expansion! Character is far more important to God than gifting. Who we are in public should be who we are in private. Integrity and honor are what God values. A person of moral excellence He values. Can you handle the criticisms that come with carrying the power of God? How about the accolades? Can you be a son or daughter He can trust with His anointing? Your mission on earth is to walk in His authority and power, but are you ready to steward that well?

*"...The Son of God appeared for this purpose, that He might destroy the works of the devil."*
**—1 John 3:8 ESV**

Do you want to be a destroyer of darkness? Do you want to be a healing agent for the hurting and downtrodden? YOU ARE THE CONDUIT GOD WANTS TO USE TO PARTNER WITH HIM TO

BRING HIS KINGDOM TO EARTH. But there is a process required to walk in this capacity, and it's called dying to our flesh. It comes through our pain points, submission, and obedience to our King.

I've learned that as God allows us to experience distress—pain, disappointment, and hardship—He's preparing a spacious place for us because character matters in representing Jesus well. The tension we experience during this growing process through pain and suffering is meant to develop our spiritual muscles. It's designed to form resistance in us, so that we can be overcomers – the devil's most feared attribute. If we submit to Jesus in the process, trusting Him with our pain, discomfort, or questions, we will GROW, ENLARGE, and become GLORY CARRIERS.

We are all called to be glory carriers, but many forfeit that privilege and mandate because they refuse to submit to the dying process. And you cannot resurrect what has not died. You have no room to contain new wine when you hold onto old ways that God wants to empty out of you. Distress will always be the catalyst to push you upward and forward, honing you, shaping you, and conforming you. Don't fear it—embrace it!

What are you withholding from the grave that is preventing your expansion? What seed are you refusing to sow? You want a fruitful harvest—you have to sow the seed. You want financial increase? Sow seeds into other people's lives and anointed ministries that God directs you to. You want marital unity and bliss? Surrender your will, your ways, and exchange your pride for humility, putting your spouse before yourself. You want Kingdom kids? Surrender control over their lives! Stop compromising yourself to them because you want to be buddies. Establish healthy boundaries so they can flourish with honor and respect. You desire restored relationships? Forgive, and then dig a 6-foot grave and place them there. Yield to the King and His promises—HE IS A GOD OF RESTORATION! He can resurrect ANYTHING.

You want the fulfillment of the dreams God has placed in your heart? Humbly give them back to Him. In His time, if they were from Him, they will be given back to you. You want prosperity of soul and health? Repent of the things you hold onto that bring destruction to your temple—addictions, food choices, laziness, trauma, hatred, pride, unforgiveness, bitterness, jealousy, lust, control. REPENT and sow them into the ground so they come back producing a fruitful crop as God flips it and turns what was rotten into something bountiful and healthy.

All things will be turned around for our good for those who love God and are called according to His purpose. Do NOT be afraid of the process of enlargement. There will be seasons of exceedingly difficult things to overcome—surrendering things you could never imagine, being called to lay it down, dying to self, killing the flesh so the spirit can live in and through you. Painful processes—but necessary.

Pressure is a catalyst for growth! God has an expansion plan just for you! If you want to truly walk in KINGDOM identity and inheritance and be His glory carrier, you MUST submit to the process of dying, take up your cross, and follow after Him.

This is God's expansion plan for your life! If you can't handle the pressure, you can't handle the next level. Allow the growth to happen. I want to leave you with this as I close out this chapter: While Christ experienced His abandonment by God, His soul rested firmly on and was fully subject to His Father. While Jesus was in His human feelings—those feelings of abandonment and pain that were ever present—Jesus held firmly to His Father!

You must know—God is your refuge in distress and your shelter in the storms and heat of life. He hears you and sees you in your distress—every tear, every fear, every question—even in your silence from doubt and unbelief, HE HEARS! HE KNOWS! But you need to know today that His plan is perfected in your weakness. In your distress, you will grow and expand if you faint not. So, in the hard places, I want to encourage you to grow in gratitude and give thanks for His tender care of you.

In **Genesis 35**, Jacob built an altar to God for delivering him from distress and to show his gratitude to the God who answered him. Allow yourself to revisit those altars—the places of remembrance in your life of His faithfulness in times past. Revisit your testimonies so that you can be encouraged in the moments of your distress. As you are stretched, it will enlarge your capacity for more of Him. The enemy wants you to forget the goodness of God, so press in and decree your victories.

# CHAPTER TWELVE

## Eye Of The Tiger: Resilient And Focused

*"So, Jeremiah, if you're worn out in this foot race
with men, what makes you think you can race against
horses? And if you can't keep your wits during times
of calm, what's going to happen when troubles break
loose like the Jordan in flood?"*
**—Jeremiah 12:5 MSG**

Have you given much thought to how you see your life
and the experiences you've encountered through the
eyes of faith? Do you ever consider the preparation it
takes to be one who has the stamina to push through
and win the race? Not just in a marathon race against
men, but as a front-runner in the Kentucky Derby?
That is what Jeremiah is describing in this scripture—
the training involved to compete and be resilient
against the stronger battles and opposing foes you will
face. To become stronger in any endeavor takes
discipline, diligence, and focus—or we will never
make it out of the gate. As we grow in spiritual
maturity and gain ground in learning the things God
teaches us through our circumstances, we become
stronger and more battle-ready.

Training is tough, but it is completely doable with the right training plan that emphasizes time and commitment, as much as it does mental and physical strength. True sons and daughters of Yahweh and heirs to His Kingdom must have the grit to train well. They need to have the eye of the tiger—an eye to *SEE* and an eye to *FIGHT*. An eye to pay attention to things around them and truly look at the deep heart of things. This is an eye that many people do not care to have—to look deeply and hunger to understand the things of the Kingdom. A deep desire to have the truth, whether people believe it or not. An eye to fight the unseen realm, which is a call to intercession—placing our ideals on the altar for His governance and will to be fulfilled in the nations.

I remember watching *Rocky III* in 1982 and feeling such empowerment, even as a young teenager, while listening to the lyrics of "Eye of the Tiger" by Survivor. Did you know that song was specifically written for that movie to represent what it means to survive and fight with passion and courage? The phrase resonates deeply with many people, as it conveys feelings of strength and tenacity, evoking images of resilience, determination, and unwavering focus. It has become a symbol of fortitude in the face of adversity and daunting odds.

I decided to do a little research about the actual eyes of tigers. I found that tigers have binocular vision that enables them to accurately assess distances and depth for maneuvering within their complex environment and stalking prey. They also have more rods (responsible for visual acuity) in their eyes than cones (responsible for color vision), which assists with night vision. This allows them to detect the movement of prey in darkness. In a similar way, we as Believers can see with our spiritual eyes and have the acuity of the Holy Spirit to detect what our natural senses miss—including that which lurks in the dark or is subtly disguised. But we must choose to yield to our spiritual senses, or discernment, so we can be sharp in the warfare we face and be in a position of offense instead of defense in our prayers. This allows us to be calm and stealth in our movements as we take on the tactics of the enemy.

It is our responsibility to allow the training of the Lord to strengthen our resolve so we can stay laser-focused and not get swayed by the hits that will come. Those hits will be the best training ground you could ever have if you put your trust in the Lord and know that He goes before you. Think about King David for a moment. Before he was king, he was just a young boy of many brothers who stayed out in the fields shepherding his flock. He was looked down upon by his older siblings and not thought of highly. But while his brothers found reasons to label him and count him as nothing, God was preparing him for so much more through the circumstances he faced out in the field. David was face-to-face with both lions and bears that would attack his flock—and he killed them all. These attacks only strengthened David's focus and resilience to one day face a greater threat—that of the giant Goliath.

If David hadn't learned to trust in God while tending to his sheep, he would have tucked tail and run. But he didn't! He persevered and knew God was with him as he fought off the attacks and became victorious in those battles. Those lessons were immensely valuable, as they built a God-confidence in him to keep his focus on the One who had his back. So, when the greater challenge arose, David already had the testimony of the God who was his deliverer. There was nothing to fear! If God had saved him from the paw of the lion and the bear, He would surely save him from the hand of the Philistine. Are you paying attention here? Some of us need to revisit those old testimonies of God's saving grace in our lives—the triumphs He's already brought us through and the victories He's already won.

I heard a quote recently that resonated with me: "Faith has a moment of release, but there's always a period of time between the 'amen'—and there it is!" Allow the battles to build you up and prepare you for the greater challenges and promotions that God wants to give you. He wants to know that He can trust you when things try to shake you up and steal your attention from Him.

I want to ask you a question: Who has your gaze? Because what you focus on, you will become. I'm going to say something that might hurt your feelings right now, but if you are not allowing yourself the privilege of the training set before you, then you are not ready to be entrusted with the next levels of kingship. Paul tells us in Philippians that he learned the secret of living in every situation—whether with a full stomach or empty, with plenty or little. He learned that he could do anything through Christ, who gives him the strength. You, my dear reader, can also do anything because of who resides in you.

You might say, "Oh, but Trena, you don't know my situation... you don't understand my struggle... you don't know the ringer I've gone through!" You are right, I do not. But He does! And there is nothing you cannot do when your gaze is set upon Him and your faith rests in His promises to you.

So, now what? What will your choices be when you are up against the wall and staring at your opponent of distraction in the eyes? What will you do when you are facing down your own lion or Goliath? Will you crumble in terror and resolve to cower down and hide from the challenge, or will you remember your prior victories and grab your sling? This path is not one to be afraid of but to embrace as the son or daughter that you are. You were built for this. God is for you. His Spirit in you is far greater than anything in this world, and He is developing you to reign with Him.

*"Consider it a sheer gift, friends, when tests and challenges come at you from all sides. You know that under pressure, your faith-life is forced into the open and shows its true colors. So don't try to get out of anything prematurely. Let it do its work so you become mature and well-developed, not deficient in any way."*
**—James 1:2-4 MSG**

I want to encourage you that there will be times of success and times when you may feel like an utter failure. The truth is, you have never truly failed at anything. You might think, "Well, Lord, I started this, but I failed at it." But God says, "NO! You think you failed, but you've learned, and you've trained yourself. I will use this for the situations that will bring success to you."

You need to just be about your Father's business and say, "God, show me, train me, help me understand this situation." He'll begin to take your apathy, sadness, and even depression, and stabilize your emotions and soul, making you stronger. Remember, it is in our weakness and sadness that we begin to find strength. When you allow this truth to override the lies, you will begin to SHIFT. And in those weak moments, He will pour out the oil of His strength upon you. Through your "I can't," you will begin declaring, "I can!" His strength will overshadow you and fill you with joy, laughter, and peace.

Everything you've been through in your life—the good, the bad, the ugly—from childhood until now, all the struggles that have tugged and pushed you this way and that way, are shaping you for this very hour. Everything you've endured has made you stronger and will continue to strengthen you as it molds you into Christlikeness.

It's time to see yourself as a warrior in God's army with the eye of the tiger. If you get knocked down, get up again. If you lose your footing, stand up and regain your balance. Learn to see what He sees and discern what He shows you. God is strong, and He has made you strong. He has provided all the weapons you need to fight, but you must put them to use. Do not let your trials be for nothing; instead, use them as training ground. Become familiar with the weapons of our warfare, because you will need them throughout your life.

This is the only way to build up stamina to resist everything the devil throws your way. You must be prepared, because you will face more than you can handle on your own—it must be in the Lord's strength with His armor covering you. Your arsenal must include knowing the Word of God, which is an indispensable weapon, and the power of prayer, a non-negotiable part of your faith journey that will grow you in intimacy with God. And intimacy with God will establish in you a backbone and an untouchable fortitude of mental strength that will lead you into victory every time.

# CONCLUSION

## The Interpretation

*"He did this because Daniel, whom the king called Belteshazzar, was found to have a keen mind and knowledge and understanding, and also the ability to interpret dreams, explain riddles, and solve difficult problems. Call for Daniel, and he will tell you what the writing means."*
—**Daniel 5:12 NIV**

Unless you cheated and jumped to the last chapter, you may have been pondering my dream since the opening pages. So here you go. This interpretation was given to me by a well-known Christian minister, dedicated educator, and recognized leader in dream interpretation.

"Trena, you have a large and expanding capacity to love and embrace others with the compassion of Christ. Your arms will be His in many sweet embraces. He will give you words to write that will convey the love and comfort of the Father toward others.

You have chosen to die to the flesh. **Galatians 5:24** says, "Now those who belong to Christ Jesus have crucified the flesh with its passions and desires." Christ is to always be exalted in our body, whether by life or by death, and "to live is Christ, and to die is gain." *Philippians 1:21.* In this "dying" process, many features will be preserved and given a new look of beauty with FAITH etched on them.

**Galatians 2:20** says, *"I have been crucified with Christ; it is no longer I who live, but Christ in me; and the life which I now live in the flesh I live by faith in the Son of God, who loved me and gave Himself up for me."* Now, it is your turn to give things up for Him. In the dream, you were submitted to the syringe. There are those aspects of Christ you will need to "inject" (declare the Word) into yourself, which will preserve you from future troubles. The look of a believer in a casket is really one of surrender and peace, in who they have now become, in their glorified bodies. And just as those in the great cloud of witnesses, you also are a "cheerleader" here on the earth for those who haven't yet "died" in some areas to become more like Him." — Great dream!

We are not called to do what makes us happy – we are called to do what glorifies God. And in this life exchange, our life for His, we are called to be set apart and made holy. The only way that happens is by our "yes" to salvation and our obedience to the Father through our daily surrender. Jesus said in **John 14**, "If you love me, you will obey me." This command is not just for when it feels good or convenient, but also when it does not make sense, when it hurts, and when we do not have all the answers. If your sacrifice does not cost you anything, it isn't a sacrifice.

I have discovered that my love for Jesus has to outweigh any other love, which I found through self-discovery in a heap of trials and through the pain of separation from loved ones. More times than I can count, I felt like I was walking in the footsteps of those in the Bible who have gone on before us, as I faced similar experiences: Joseph's rejection and betrayal from family, Abraham's excruciating decision to sacrifice his own child, whom he had loved dearly and waited his whole life for. And Job...oh Job! Loving God and yet being stripped of what seemed like everything important in my life. These lovers of God had a choice to trust Him. God either was who He said He was, or He was a liar! You have a choice, too. If God is for you, then who can be against you?

*"Come to God through the narrow gate, because the wide gate and broad path is the way that leads to destruction – nearly everyone chooses that crowded road! The narrow gate and the difficult way leads to eternal life – so few even find it!"*
**—Matthew 7:13 TPT**

I want you to know that this life of surrender is not as difficult as we have been led to believe. Yes, it will have its challenges, and you will cry rivers of tears. Some of you may have experienced unimaginable trauma from wickedness in degrees that deserve nothing less than execution. Some have felt deep shame engulf them from the enemy's schemes. You must know to the depths of your being that God will take all that pain and use what the enemy tried to take you out with, for your purpose on this earth. Never allow the devil to shame you out of your testimony! Do you know anyone else in the entire universe who you can trust like God Almighty, who set the boundaries of the oceans and placed the stars in the sky?

My hope is that you learn this life lesson and the deeper revelations to this key to an abundant Kingdom life; one that will forge a path of genuine repentance, spiritual growth that transcends your family line, and breakthrough over your life. I can wholeheartedly say to you, with Christ, you got this. Our modern-day comforts and societal upside-down thinking that we have been inundated with may tell us otherwise, but the truth is that a surrendered life just requires a genuine relationship with Jesus, faith as small as a mustard seed, and an obedient heart. Think of how a child fully depends upon its parent for every need it has, whether material things or provision and security. With healthy parents, every need is met for that child. It is the same for us who look to the Father for our every need. But along the way of holding that parent's hand and fully trusting them, we also find ourselves corrected or disciplined when we veer the wrong way. Not because they wanted to harm us, but protect us. God does the same for us, but with absolute love, divine counsel, and wisdom. There is nobody else you can fully trust your life with but Him. You are safe in His covering, and know He has the very best plans prepared for you. This is that narrow road, and it is the one you want to be found on, but it will require grit, so do not despise the perseverance it shapes in you and the passion that comes through suffering to stay on it. His foundations are being laid in your life, and although the building goes up quickly, the foundation that it sits on takes a much longer time to engineer and lay so that it can hold the structure soundly.

This book was meant to give you hope through your faith journey and to help you shave off years of fear and frustration to let go and let God. He is your safe place. I know it sounds cliché, but there really is purpose in our pain. If you put your trust in Him, God will orchestrate divine reversal and jettison you into your destiny on this earth. Take the counsel of the words in this book to be a road map for you to shorten that trip around the mountain. Because trust me, nobody wants to take forty years to complete what could be done in two weeks. Just know that if it does take years, that too is okay. God is refining you and aligning others in this process, and in His perfect timing, if you remain steadfast, you will arise from the heap of ashes without smelling like smoke.

You may be asking, "But how? How do I do this surrender thing? How do I really trust the Lover of my soul?" There is no easy answer other than to just do it. Do what the Word tells you to do. Have faith. Trust Him. Obey Him. Along the way, as you grow in intimacy in your relationship with Jesus, it becomes easier because you know Him better. The more you know Him in Word and in fellowship, the more you realize how majestic His covering is over you, and trusting Him becomes the byproduct of that union. As you learn to embrace the journey of carrying your cross and giving your life as a living sacrifice, you will become deeply familiar with the ending of the story. God wins! That means you win!

So, grab the bull by the horns and decide today to ride out all the forces against you and to place all your bets on the future and hope He has prepared for you before the beginning of time. Have confidence knowing that if you are under the Spirit of God, the devil cannot touch you. This is the process He has chosen for His bride, who are being made holy as He is holy. Jesus' return is coming, and the Church must be equipped with The Truth and the understanding of the power of our surrender so we can be that spotless, beautiful bride prepared for her groom with our lamps full of oil. I encourage you to be steadfast in knowing that God's mighty power is perfected in the face of our hardships because when we are weak, He is strong. Jesus is not looking for your perfection; He's looking for your surrender.

The Church is at the cusp of family revival — let's rise, breaking every stronghold of resistance over our households, and usher in a generation of wholeness that is pleasing to the Lord. Today is the day to turn your heart fully to Him and embrace your story. It's your time, valiant warrior, to rattle the gates of hell with your full surrender and confound every enemy with your, "Yes, Lord, not my will, but Yours be done."

Never forget that faith, surrender, and obedience hold the key to your breakthrough. Walk confidently knowing that when you embrace these things, you are then seeking first the Kingdom, and all other things will be added to you. Welcome to the fully abundant, transformational, bondage-breaking powerhouse of the inherited life of Kingdom Living!

To find out more about Trena and her ministry, you can visit her online:

Website: www.lifebuildernetwork.com

Facebook: www.facebook.com/lifebuildernetwork

Instagram: @lifebuildernetwork

www.ingramcontent.com/pod-product-compliance
Lightning Source LLC
Chambersburg PA
CBHW061651120626
46550CB00003B/900